Ink and Hea

Transformative Teaching
Where Emotions Meet Chalk
Dust

While every precaution has been taken in the preparation of this book, the publisher assumes no responsibility for errors or omissions, or for damages resulting from the use of the information contained herein.

INK AND HEART: A GUIDE TO TRANSFORMATIVE TEACHING

First edition. November 23, 2023.

Written by imed el arbi.

Table of Contents

Transformative Teaching: Emotions, Connection, Growth. Explore the power of emotions in education, creating a safe classroom environment, fostering connection, and nurturing personal transformation. Discover strategies for emotional intelligence, inclusivity, meaningful learning experiences, and conflict resolution. Embrace lifelong learning and student-centered approaches. Ignite curiosity, passion, and intrinsic motivation.

Introduction:

Ink and Heart: A Guide to Transformative Teaching Where Emotions Meet Chalk Dust

In the hallowed halls of education, where sunlight dances through classroom windows and whispers echo off ancient chalkboards, there exists a quiet revolution. It's not about rigid curricula or standardized tests; it's about something deeper—a symphony of ink and heart.

Welcome to "Ink and Heart," a compass for educators navigating uncharted seas. Within these pages lies a world where emotions are not distractions but essential companions on the learning voyage. It is here that we embark on a journey to explore the art of teaching resilience, empathy, and self-awareness—the invisible threads that weave a safety net for students' hearts.

Education is not solely about imparting knowledge; it is about shaping lives, nurturing young minds, and fostering growth. As teachers, we hold the power to create transformative experiences that extend far beyond the boundaries of the classroom. We have the opportunity to touch the very core of a student's being, to ignite their passion for learning, and to empower them to become compassionate, resilient individuals.

"Ink and Heart" is a guide that seeks to bridge the gap between the intellectual and the emotional aspects of education. It recognizes that a student's heart and mind are intimately intertwined and that true learning occurs when both are engaged. It is a call to action, an invitation to embrace a teaching approach that not only imparts knowledge but also nurtures the soul.

Within these chapters, we will embark on a profound exploration of transformative teaching practices. We will delve into the importance of fostering emotional intelligence, cultivating empathy, and creating a safe and inclusive learning environment. We will discover ways to encourage self-reflection and self-expression, allowing students to discover their unique voices and identities.

Through the power of storytelling, we will encounter real-life examples of teachers who have made a lasting impact on their students' lives. Their tales will inspire and illuminate the path ahead, reminding us of the immense influence we possess as educators. We will unravel the secrets of building meaningful connections with students and fostering a sense of belonging and trust that paves the way for authentic learning experiences.

"Ink and Heart" is not a prescriptive manual; it is a tapestry of ideas, insights, and strategies that can be woven into the fabric of any classroom. Each teacher brings their own unique strengths and passions, and this book encourages you to embrace your individuality while providing a rich tapestry of tools to enhance your practice.

As you embark on this journey through the pages of "Ink and Heart," open your mind and heart to the possibilities that lie ahead. Be prepared to challenge conventional wisdom, to embrace vulnerability, and to champion the potential within each and every student. Together, let us reimagine education as a transformative force—one where emotions and intellect entwine and the ink of knowledge merges with the boundless depths of the human heart.

So, let us set sail on this voyage together—a voyage that transcends the confines of a syllabus and invites us to embark on a lifelong pursuit of growth, compassion, and wisdom. Welcome to "Ink and Heart: A Guide to Transformative Teaching," where emotions meet chalk dust and classrooms become sanctuaries of learning, empathy, and profound connection.

Chapter 1: The Palette of Emotions

1.1 Understanding Emotions

E motions are an integral part of the human experience. They shape our thoughts, actions, and interactions with others. In the context of teaching, understanding emotions is crucial for creating a supportive and engaging learning environment. When teachers have a deep understanding of emotions, they can effectively connect with their students, foster positive relationships, and facilitate meaningful learning experiences.

The Complexity of Emotions

EMOTIONS ARE COMPLEX and multifaceted. They can range from simple feelings like happiness and sadness to more nuanced emotions such as anger, fear, and surprise. Each emotion carries its own unique set of physiological and psychological responses. For example, when a student feels anxious, their heart rate may increase, their palms may become sweaty, and their thoughts may become scattered.

The Importance of Emotional Awareness

EMOTIONAL AWARENESS is the foundation for understanding emotions. It involves recognizing and acknowledging one's own emotions as well as the emotions of others. As a teacher, being emotionally aware allows you to empathize with your students, understand their needs, and respond appropriately. It also helps you recognize the impact of your own emotions on your teaching practice.

The Role of Emotional Intelligence

EMOTIONAL INTELLIGENCE refers to the ability to recognize, understand, and manage one's own emotions as well as the emotions of others. It encompasses skills such as self-awareness, self-regulation, empathy, and social skills. In the context of teaching, emotional intelligence plays a vital role in building positive relationships with students, resolving conflicts, and creating a supportive classroom environment.

Developing Emotional Intelligence in Teaching

DEVELOPING EMOTIONAL intelligence in teaching requires self-reflection and a commitment to personal growth. It involves becoming aware of your own emotions, understanding their triggers, and learning strategies to regulate them effectively. It also involves developing empathy and understanding the perspectives and emotions of your students.

The Benefits of Emotional Regulation

EMOTIONAL REGULATION refers to the ability to manage and control one's emotions in a healthy and constructive manner. It is an essential skill for both teachers and students. When teachers can regulate their emotions, they can create a calm and focused learning environment. Similarly, when students learn to regulate their emotions, they can better engage in learning and develop resilience.

Strategies for emotional regulation

THERE ARE VARIOUS STRATEGIES that teachers can employ to promote emotional regulation in the classroom. These strategies include:

1. Mindfulness: Practicing mindfulness exercises can help teachers and students become more aware of their emotions and develop the ability to respond rather than react impulsively.
2. Breathing exercises: Teaching students simple breathing techniques can help them calm their minds and bodies during moments of stress or anxiety.
3. Emotional check-ins: Allocating time for students to express their emotions and concerns can help them feel heard and supported.
4. Journaling: Encouraging students to keep a journal where they can reflect on their emotions and experiences can promote self-awareness and emotional regulation.
5. Positive self-talk: Teaching students to reframe negative thoughts and replace them with positive affirmations can help them manage their emotions more effectively.

Creating an Emotionally Safe Classroom Environment

AN EMOTIONALLY SAFE classroom environment is one where students feel comfortable expressing their emotions, taking risks, and making mistakes. It is a space where students are respected, valued, and supported. Creating such an environment requires:

1. Building positive relationships: Developing strong relationships with students based on trust and respect is essential for creating an emotionally safe classroom.
2. Establishing clear expectations: Setting clear expectations for behavior and communication helps students feel secure and know what is expected of them.
3. Encouraging open communication: Creating opportunities for students to express their thoughts and emotions openly without fear of judgment or ridicule fosters a sense of safety and belonging.
4. Providing support and resources: Offering support and resources to students who may be struggling emotionally helps create a supportive and inclusive classroom environment.

Understanding emotions is a fundamental aspect of transformative teaching. By developing emotional intelligence, practicing emotional regulation, and creating an emotionally safe classroom environment, teachers can cultivate a positive and engaging learning experience for their students. In the following chapters, we will explore additional tools and strategies for heartfelt teaching that build upon this understanding of emotions.

1.2 Emotional Intelligence in Teaching

EMOTIONAL INTELLIGENCE is a crucial aspect of teaching that goes beyond subject knowledge and pedagogical skills. It involves the ability to understand and manage one's own emotions as well as the emotions of others. In the context of teaching, emotional intelligence plays a significant role in creating a positive and supportive learning environment, building strong relationships with students, and promoting their social and emotional development.

The Importance of Emotional Intelligence in Teaching

TEACHING IS NOT JUST about imparting knowledge; it is about connecting with students on a deeper level and understanding their individual needs and emotions. Emotional intelligence allows teachers to empathize with their students, recognize their emotional states, and respond appropriately. When teachers are emotionally intelligent, they can create a safe and nurturing environment where students feel valued, understood, and supported.

Understanding Emotions in the Classroom

EMOTIONS ARE AN INTEGRAL part of the learning process. Students come to the classroom with a wide range of emotions, influenced by various factors such as personal experiences, relationships, and external stressors. As a teacher, it is essential to recognize and acknowledge these emotions, both positive and negative, and create a space where students feel comfortable expressing themselves.

By understanding the emotions of students, teachers can tailor their teaching approaches to meet their needs effectively. For example, if a student is feeling anxious, the teacher can provide additional support and reassurance. On the other hand, if a student is feeling excited, the teacher can channel that energy into productive learning activities.

Developing Emotional Intelligence as a Teacher

EMOTIONAL INTELLIGENCE is not a fixed trait; it can be developed and enhanced over time. As a teacher, there are several strategies you can employ to cultivate your emotional intelligence:

Self-reflection and self-awareness

START BY REFLECTING on your own emotions and how they impact your teaching. Take the time to understand your strengths and weaknesses in managing emotions. By becoming more self-aware, you can better regulate your emotions and respond effectively to challenging situations in the classroom.

Active listening and empathy

ACTIVE LISTENING INVOLVES not only hearing what students say but also understanding their emotions and perspectives. Practice empathetic listening by putting yourself in their shoes and trying to understand their experiences. This will help you build stronger connections with your students and create a supportive learning environment.

Emotional regulation techniques

TEACHING CAN BE A DEMANDING profession, and it is essential to have strategies in place to regulate your own emotions. Deep breathing exercises, mindfulness techniques, and taking short breaks can help you manage stress and maintain a calm and composed demeanor in the classroom.

Continuous Professional Development

INVEST IN YOUR OWN professional development to enhance your emotional intelligence. Attend workshops, conferences, and training sessions that focus on social and emotional learning. Engage in discussions with other educators to learn from their experiences and gain new insights into effective teaching practices.

Applying Emotional Intelligence in the Classroom

ONCE YOU HAVE DEVELOPED your emotional intelligence as a teacher, you can apply it in various ways to create a positive and supportive classroom environment:

Building positive relationships

EMOTIONAL INTELLIGENCE allows you to build strong and positive relationships with your students. By understanding their emotions and needs, you can establish trust and create a sense of belonging. This, in turn, fosters a supportive learning environment where students feel comfortable taking risks and engaging in meaningful discussions.

Effective Communication

EMOTIONAL INTELLIGENCE enables you to communicate effectively with your students. By being aware of their emotions, you can adapt your communication style to ensure clarity and understanding. You can also use non-verbal cues and body language to convey empathy and support.

Conflict Resolution

CONFLICTS ARE INEVITABLE in any classroom setting. However, with emotional intelligence, you can effectively manage and resolve conflicts. By understanding the emotions underlying the conflict, you can facilitate open and respectful discussions, helping students find common ground and reach a resolution.

Promoting social and emotional learning

EMOTIONAL INTELLIGENCE is closely linked to social and emotional learning (SEL). By incorporating SEL strategies into your teaching, you can help students develop self-awareness, self-management, social awareness, relationship skills, and responsible decision-making. This holistic approach to education nurtures the whole child and prepares them for success in both academics and life.

In conclusion, emotional intelligence is a vital skill for teachers to possess. It allows them to create a positive and supportive learning environment, build strong relationships with students, and promote their social and emotional development. By developing their emotional intelligence, teachers can effectively understand and manage their own emotions as well as the emotions of their students, leading to transformative teaching experiences.

1.3 Emotional Regulation Strategies

EMOTIONS ARE AN INTEGRAL part of the human experience, and they play a significant role in the teaching and learning process. As an educator, it is essential to understand and acknowledge the emotions that arise within yourself and your students. However, it is equally important to develop strategies for regulating these emotions effectively. In this section, we will explore various emotional regulation strategies that can help create a harmonious and productive classroom environment.

1.3.1 Recognizing and Labeling Emotions

THE FIRST STEP IN EMOTIONAL regulation is to recognize and label the emotions that arise within ourselves and our students. By acknowledging and understanding our emotions, we can better manage them. Encourage your students to identify and express their feelings by creating a safe and non-judgmental space for open communication. Teach them emotional vocabulary and provide them with tools to express their emotions effectively. By doing so, you empower your students to regulate their emotions and develop emotional intelligence.

1.3.2 Deep Breathing and Mindfulness

DEEP BREATHING AND mindfulness techniques are powerful tools for emotional regulation. Encourage your students to take deep breaths when they feel overwhelmed or anxious. Teach them simple mindfulness exercises, such as focusing on their breath or observing their surroundings without judgment. These practices help calm the mind, reduce stress, and promote emotional well-being. Incorporate short mindfulness activities into your daily routine to create a sense of calm and centeredness in the classroom.

1.3.3 Physical Movement and Exercise

PHYSICAL MOVEMENT AND exercise have a profound impact on our emotional state. Encourage your students to engage in regular physical activity, whether it's through structured physical education classes or short movement breaks throughout the day. Physical movement releases endorphins, which are natural mood boosters. It also helps reduce stress and anxiety. Incorporate movement-based activities into your lessons to promote emotional regulation and enhance overall well-being.

1.3.4 Journaling and Self-Reflection

JOURNALING AND SELF-reflection provide an outlet for students to process their emotions and gain self-awareness. Encourage your students to keep a journal where they can write about their thoughts, feelings, and experiences. Provide prompts that encourage self-reflection and introspection. By engaging in this practice, students can better understand their emotions, identify patterns, and develop strategies for emotional regulation. Additionally, journaling can serve as a valuable tool for you as an educator to gain insights into your students' emotional well-being.

1.3.5 Creating a Calming Environment

THE PHYSICAL ENVIRONMENT plays a significant role in emotional regulation. Create a calming and nurturing classroom environment that promotes emotional well-being. Consider factors such as lighting, colors, and seating arrangements. Provide comfortable spaces where students can retreat when they need a moment to regulate their emotions. Incorporate elements of nature, such as plants or natural light, to create a soothing atmosphere. By designing a calming environment, you provide your students with a safe space to regulate their emotions effectively.

1.3.6 Teaching Coping Skills

TEACHING STUDENTS COPING skills equips them with the tools they need to navigate challenging emotions and situations. Introduce various coping strategies, such as deep breathing, positive self-talk, visualization, and problem-solving techniques. Teach your students how to identify triggers and develop personalized coping mechanisms. By empowering your students with these skills, you enable them to regulate their emotions independently and build resilience.

1.3.7 Modeling Emotional Regulation

AS AN EDUCATOR, YOU serve as a role model for your students. Model healthy emotional regulation by openly expressing and managing your own emotions. Demonstrate effective coping strategies when faced with challenging situations. By modeling emotional regulation, you create a safe and supportive environment where students feel comfortable exploring and regulating their own emotions.

1.3.8 Seeking Support

RECOGNIZE THAT EMOTIONAL regulation is an ongoing process, and it is essential to seek support when needed. Encourage your students to reach out to trusted adults, such as parents, counselors, or teachers, when they require assistance with emotional regulation. Foster a culture of support and empathy within the classroom where students feel comfortable seeking help. Additionally, as an educator, prioritize your own well-being and seek support from colleagues or professional development opportunities to enhance your emotional regulation skills.

By implementing these emotional regulation strategies, you create a classroom environment that supports the emotional well-being of both yourself and your students. Remember that emotional regulation is a lifelong skill, and by cultivating it in the classroom, you empower your students to navigate their emotions effectively and thrive academically and personally.

1.4 Creating an Emotionally Safe Classroom Environment

CREATING AN EMOTIONALLY safe classroom environment is essential for fostering a positive and conducive learning atmosphere. When students feel emotionally safe, they are more likely to engage in learning, take risks, and develop meaningful connections with their peers and teachers. In this section, we will explore strategies and practices that can help teachers create an emotionally safe classroom environment.

1.4.1 Establishing Clear Expectations and Boundaries

ONE OF THE FIRST STEPS in creating an emotionally safe classroom environment is establishing clear expectations and boundaries. When students know what is expected of them and understand the boundaries of acceptable behavior, they feel more secure and confident in their learning environment. Teachers can achieve this by clearly communicating their expectations and rules at the beginning of the school year or semester. It is important to involve students in the process by discussing and collaboratively setting classroom norms and rules. This not only helps students feel a sense of ownership but also promotes a shared responsibility for maintaining a safe and respectful classroom environment.

1.4.2 Building Positive Relationships

BUILDING POSITIVE RELATIONSHIPS with students is another crucial aspect of creating an emotionally safe classroom environment. When students feel valued, respected, and cared for, they are more likely to feel safe and supported in their learning journey. Teachers can foster positive relationships by taking the time to get to know their students on a personal level, showing genuine interest in their lives, and actively listening to their thoughts and concerns. Additionally, incorporating activities that promote teamwork, collaboration, and empathy can help students develop strong bonds with their peers, further enhancing the overall classroom environment.

1.4.3 Encouraging Open Communication

OPEN COMMUNICATION is key to creating an emotionally safe classroom environment. Teachers should encourage students to express their thoughts, feelings, and concerns openly and without fear of judgment. This can be achieved by creating a safe space for dialogue where students feel comfortable sharing their ideas and opinions. Teachers can also model effective communication by actively listening to students, validating their experiences, and responding empathetically. By fostering open communication, teachers can create an environment where students feel heard, understood, and supported.

1.4.4 Promoting Emotional Literacy

PROMOTING EMOTIONAL literacy is an essential component of creating an emotionally safe classroom environment. When students have a strong understanding of their own emotions and the emotions of others, they are better equipped to navigate social interactions and manage their own emotional well-being. Teachers can incorporate activities and discussions that help students identify and label their emotions, understand the causes and effects of different emotions, and develop strategies for regulating their emotions. By promoting emotional literacy, teachers empower students to express themselves authentically and develop healthy coping mechanisms.

1.4.5 Cultivating a Culture of Respect and Acceptance

CREATING AN EMOTIONALLY safe classroom environment requires cultivating a culture of respect and acceptance. Teachers should foster an inclusive environment where diversity is celebrated and differences are embraced. This can be achieved by incorporating diverse perspectives and experiences into the curriculum, promoting empathy and understanding, and addressing issues of bias and discrimination. Teachers should also model respectful behavior and encourage students to treat one another with kindness and empathy. By cultivating a culture of respect and acceptance, teachers create an environment where all students feel valued and included.

1.4.6 Addressing Conflict and Bullying

ADDRESSING CONFLICT and bullying is crucial for maintaining an emotionally safe classroom environment.

Teachers should have clear protocols in place for addressing conflicts and incidents of bullying promptly and effectively. It is important to create a safe reporting system where students can confidentially report incidents and seek support. Teachers should also provide opportunities for conflict resolution and teach students strategies for resolving conflicts peacefully. By addressing conflict and bullying head-on, teachers create a safe and supportive environment where students can thrive.

1.4.7 Providing Support and Resources

CREATING AN EMOTIONALLY safe classroom environment also involves providing support and resources for students who may be struggling emotionally. Teachers should be aware of the signs of emotional distress and be prepared to offer appropriate support or refer students to the necessary resources. This may include collaborating with school counselors, social workers, or other support staff to ensure students receive the help they need. By providing support and resources, teachers demonstrate their commitment to the well-being of their students and create an environment where students feel supported and cared for.

In conclusion, creating an emotionally safe classroom environment is essential for promoting student well-being, engagement, and academic success. By establishing clear expectations and boundaries, building positive relationships, encouraging open communication, promoting emotional literacy, cultivating a culture of respect and acceptance, addressing conflict and bullying, and providing support and resources, teachers can create an environment where students feel safe, valued, and empowered to learn and grow.

Chapter 2: Tools for Heartfelt Teaching

2.1 Building Relationships with Students

B uilding strong relationships with students is the foundation of transformative teaching. When students feel valued, understood, and connected to their teacher, they are more likely to engage in the learning process and achieve academic success. In this section, we will explore strategies and techniques for building meaningful relationships with students.

2.1.1 Creating a Welcoming Classroom Environment

THE FIRST STEP IN BUILDING relationships with students is creating a welcoming and inclusive classroom environment. This involves setting clear expectations for behavior, creating a safe space for students to express themselves, and fostering a sense of belonging. Teachers can achieve this by:

- Greeting students at the door: Welcoming students with a smile and a personal greeting sets a positive tone for the day and shows students that they are valued.

• Arranging the classroom layout: Creating a comfortable and inviting physical space can help students feel at ease and ready to learn.

• Establishing classroom norms: Collaboratively developing a set of rules and expectations with students promotes a sense of ownership and accountability.

• Celebrating diversity: Recognizing and appreciating the unique backgrounds and experiences of students helps create an inclusive environment where everyone feels respected and valued.

2.1.2 Getting to Know Your Students

TO BUILD STRONG RELATIONSHIPS with students, it is essential to get to know them on a personal level. This involves understanding their interests, strengths, challenges, and cultural backgrounds. Here are some strategies for getting to know your students:

• Conducting interest surveys: Administering surveys or questionnaires that ask students about their hobbies, favorite subjects, and goals can provide valuable insights into their individual interests and aspirations.

• Engaging in one-on-one conversations: Taking the time to have individual conversations with students allows teachers to learn more about their unique experiences, challenges, and aspirations.

• Using icebreaker activities: Incorporating icebreaker activities into the classroom routine can help students feel more comfortable sharing information about themselves and getting to know their peers.

2.1.3 Building Trust and Rapport

TRUST AND RAPPORT ARE crucial elements of any successful teacher-student relationship. When students trust their teacher, they are more likely to take risks, ask questions, and seek support. Here are some strategies for building trust and rapport with students:

• Be authentic and genuine: Students can sense when a teacher is being authentic and genuinely cares about their well-being. Show empathy, listen actively, and be responsive to their needs.

• Maintain confidentiality: Respecting students' privacy and maintaining confidentiality when they share personal information or concerns is essential for building trust.

• Show interest in their lives: Take an interest in students' lives outside of the classroom by asking about their hobbies, extracurricular activities, and family. This demonstrates that you value them as individuals, not just as students.

• Provide support and encouragement: Offer praise and constructive feedback to help students build confidence and feel supported in their learning journey.

2.1.4 Cultivating Positive Teacher-Student Relationships

POSITIVE TEACHER-STUDENT relationships are built on mutual respect, understanding, and effective communication. Here are some strategies for cultivating positive relationships with students:

• Use positive language: Encourage and uplift students by using positive language and affirmations. Avoid negative or derogatory comments that can undermine their self-esteem.

• Be approachable and available. Create opportunities for students to seek help or guidance by being approachable and available during and outside of class time.

• Incorporate student voice and choice: involve students in decision-making processes and provide opportunities for them to have a say in their learning. This fosters a sense of ownership and empowerment.

- Show appreciation: recognize and celebrate students' achievements, both big and small. This helps foster a positive classroom culture and reinforces their efforts.

Building relationships with students takes time and effort, but the rewards are immeasurable. When students feel connected to their teacher, they are more likely to be engaged, motivated, and successful in their academic pursuits. By creating a welcoming environment, getting to know your students, building trust and rapport, and cultivating positive relationships, you can lay the groundwork for transformative teaching that leaves a lasting impact on students' lives.

2.2 Effective Communication Techniques

EFFECTIVE COMMUNICATION is the cornerstone of any successful teaching practice. It is through clear and meaningful communication that teachers can establish rapport with their students, foster a positive classroom environment, and facilitate learning. In this section, we will explore various communication techniques that can help teachers enhance their effectiveness in the classroom.

2.2.1 Verbal Communication

VERBAL COMMUNICATION is the most common form of communication in the classroom. It involves the use of spoken words to convey information, instructions, and ideas. To ensure effective verbal communication, teachers should consider the following techniques:

1. Clarity and Conciseness: It is important for teachers to speak clearly and concisely, using language that is appropriate for the age and comprehension level of their students. Avoid using jargon or complex vocabulary that may confuse students.
2. Tone and Intonation: The tone and intonation of a teacher's voice can greatly impact how their message is received. Using a warm and friendly tone can help create a positive classroom atmosphere, while varying the intonation can make the delivery of information more engaging.
3. Active Listening: Effective communication is a two-

way process. Teachers should actively listen to their students, giving them their full attention and responding appropriately. This not only shows respect for the students but also encourages them to participate and engage in the learning process.

4. Non-Verbal Cues: Non-verbal cues, such as facial expressions, gestures, and body language, can enhance the effectiveness of verbal communication. Teachers should be mindful of their own non-verbal cues and also be observant of their students' non-verbal cues to gauge their understanding and engagement.

2.2.2 Written Communication

WRITTEN COMMUNICATION plays a significant role in teaching, especially when it comes to providing instructions, giving feedback, and documenting students' progress. Here are some techniques to enhance written communication:

1. Clarity and Organization: When writing instructions or providing feedback, it is essential to be clear and organized. Use simple and concise language, break down complex information into smaller parts, and use headings or bullet points to make the text more readable.

2. Timeliness: Providing timely written feedback and updates is crucial for students to stay on track and feel supported. Teachers should establish a system for regular communication, whether it be through written progress reports, emails, or online platforms.

3. Visual Aids: Incorporating visual aids, such as charts,

diagrams, or infographics, can enhance written communication by making information more accessible and engaging. Visual aids can help students understand complex concepts, remember key information, and make connections between different ideas.

4. Digital Tools: With the advancement of technology, teachers have access to a wide range of digital tools that can facilitate written communication. These tools include online platforms for sharing assignments and feedback, collaborative writing platforms, and multimedia presentation tools.

2.2.3 Non-Verbal Communication

NON-VERBAL COMMUNICATION refers to the use of body language, facial expressions, and gestures to convey messages without words. It is an essential aspect of effective communication in the classroom. Here are some techniques to consider:

1. Eye Contact: Maintaining eye contact with students while speaking or listening shows attentiveness and respect. It helps establish a connection and encourages students to actively participate in discussions.

2. Facial Expressions: Facial expressions can convey a range of emotions and can greatly impact how students perceive and interpret messages. Smiling, nodding, and showing empathy through facial expressions can create a positive and supportive

classroom environment.

3. Body Language: Teachers should be aware of their body language and use it intentionally to enhance communication. Open and relaxed postures can signal approachability, while moving around the classroom can help maintain students' attention and engagement.

4. Proximity: Physical proximity can be used strategically to communicate with students. Moving closer to a student who needs assistance or standing near a group of students during a collaborative activity can signal support and involvement.

2.2.4 Digital Communication

IN TODAY'S DIGITAL age, teachers often need to communicate with students and parents through digital platforms. Here are some techniques for effective digital communication:

1. Clear and succinct messages: When communicating through digital platforms, it is important to keep messages clear, concise, and to the point. Avoid using excessive jargon or technical terms that may confuse recipients.

2. Use of Multimedia: Digital communication allows for the use of multimedia elements such as images, videos, and audio recordings. Incorporating these elements can make messages more engaging and help convey information more effectively.

3. Privacy and Security: When communicating digitally,

teachers must prioritize the privacy and security of their students. Ensure that communication platforms are secure and adhere to privacy regulations. Use appropriate channels for sensitive information and obtain consent when necessary.

4. Timely Responses: Just as with written communication, timely responses are crucial in digital communication. Students and parents should feel that their messages are valued and that their concerns are being addressed promptly.

By employing these effective communication techniques, teachers can create a positive and inclusive classroom environment, foster strong relationships with their students, and facilitate meaningful learning experiences. Communication is not just about transmitting information; it is about connecting with students on an emotional level and empowering them to become active participants in their own education.

2.3 Active listening and empathy

ACTIVE LISTENING AND empathy are two essential skills that can greatly enhance the teaching experience and create a positive and supportive classroom environment. As a teacher, it is crucial to not only impart knowledge but also to understand and connect with your students on a deeper level. Active listening involves fully engaging with what the students are saying, while empathy allows you to understand and share their feelings and experiences. Together, these skills can foster trust, build relationships, and promote effective communication within the classroom.

The Power of Active Listening

ACTIVE LISTENING IS more than just hearing what someone is saying; it involves giving your full attention and being present in the moment. When you actively listen to your students, you show them that their thoughts and opinions are valued. This can boost their confidence and encourage them to participate more actively in class discussions.

To practice active listening, start by maintaining eye contact with the student who is speaking. This shows that you are fully engaged and interested in what they have to say. Avoid interrupting or finishing their sentences, as this can make them feel unheard or dismissed. Instead, allow them to express their thoughts fully before responding.

Another important aspect of active listening is paraphrasing or summarizing what the student has said. This not only demonstrates that you have understood their message but also gives them an opportunity to clarify or expand on their ideas. Reflecting back on their words also shows that you are actively processing and internalizing their thoughts.

Active listening can also be enhanced through non-verbal cues such as nodding, smiling, or using facial expressions that convey understanding and empathy. These gestures can help create a safe and supportive environment where students feel comfortable expressing themselves.

Cultivating empathy in the classroom

EMPATHY IS THE ABILITY to understand and share the feelings of another person. It is a crucial skill for teachers to possess, as it allows them to connect with their students on a deeper level and create a sense of belonging in the classroom. When students feel understood and valued, they are more likely to engage in the learning process and develop a positive attitude towards education.

To cultivate empathy in the classroom, it is important to create opportunities for students to share their thoughts, feelings, and experiences. This can be done through class discussions, journaling exercises, or small group activities. Encourage students to listen to and respect each other's perspectives, fostering an environment of empathy and understanding.

As a teacher, it is also important to model empathy in your interactions with students. Show genuine interest in their lives, ask open-ended questions, and actively listen to their responses. By demonstrating empathy, you create a safe space where students feel comfortable expressing themselves and seeking support when needed.

Incorporating literature and storytelling into your teaching can also be a powerful tool for developing empathy. By exploring different characters' experiences and emotions, students can gain a deeper understanding of diverse perspectives and develop empathy towards others.

The Benefits of Active Listening and Empathy

ACTIVE LISTENING AND empathy have numerous benefits for both teachers and students. When teachers actively listen to their students, they gain valuable insights into their needs, interests, and learning styles. This allows teachers to tailor their instruction to meet individual student needs, promoting a more inclusive and effective learning environment.

Active listening and empathy also foster stronger relationships between teachers and students. When students feel heard and understood, they are more likely to trust and respect their teachers. This positive teacher-student relationship can lead to increased student engagement, motivation, and academic success.

Furthermore, active listening and empathy can help resolve conflicts and address behavioral issues in the classroom. By understanding the underlying emotions and motivations behind student behavior, teachers can respond in a compassionate and supportive manner, promoting positive behavior and emotional growth.

In conclusion, active listening and empathy are essential skills for transformative teaching. By actively listening to your students and cultivating empathy in the classroom, you can create a supportive and inclusive learning environment where students feel valued and understood. These skills not only enhance communication and relationships but also promote academic success and emotional well-being. As a teacher, embracing active listening and empathy can truly make a difference in the lives of your students.

Chapter 3 : The Rainbow of SEL (Social Emotional Learning)

3.1 Introduction to SEL

Social Emotional Learning (SEL) is a powerful framework that focuses on developing the social and emotional skills of students, enabling them to navigate the complexities of life with resilience, empathy, and self-awareness. In this chapter, we will explore the fundamental principles of SEL and their significance in transformative teaching.

3.1.1 Understanding SEL

SEL ENCOMPASSES A RANGE of skills and competencies that enable individuals to understand and manage their emotions, establish and maintain positive relationships, make responsible decisions, and demonstrate empathy and compassion towards others. It recognizes that emotional well-being and social skills are essential for academic success and overall personal growth.

At its core, SEL aims to cultivate a supportive and inclusive learning environment where students feel safe, valued, and empowered to express themselves authentically. By integrating SEL into teaching practices, educators can foster a holistic approach to education that nurtures the hearts and minds of their students.

3.1.2 The Five Core Competencies of SEL

SEL IS BUILT UPON FIVE core competencies that provide a framework for developing emotional intelligence and social skills in students. These competencies are:

1. **Self-awareness**: This competency involves recognizing and understanding one's emotions, strengths, and weaknesses. It also includes developing a positive self-image and a sense of personal identity.

2. **Self-Management**: Self-management focuses on regulating emotions, controlling impulses, and setting and achieving goals. It involves developing strategies for stress management, self-motivation, and perseverance.

3. **Social Awareness**: Social awareness encompasses the ability to understand and empathize with others' emotions, perspectives, and experiences. It involves developing skills such as active listening, empathy, and cultural sensitivity.

4. **Relationship Skills**: Relationship skills involve building and maintaining healthy relationships, resolving conflicts, and effectively communicating with others. It includes skills such as teamwork, cooperation, and effective communication.

5. **Responsible Decision-Making**: Responsible decision-making involves making ethical and constructive choices based on consideration of social norms, safety concerns, and the well-being of oneself and others. It includes skills such as problem-solving, critical thinking, and ethical reasoning.

3.1.3 The Benefits of SEL

INTEGRATING SEL INTO teaching practices offers numerous benefits for both students and educators. Some of the key benefits include:

1. **Improved Academic Performance**: SEL provides a strong foundation for academic success by enhancing students' ability to focus, manage their time effectively, and engage in critical thinking and problem-solving.

2. **Enhanced Emotional Well-Being**: SEL equips students with the skills to understand and manage their emotions, reducing stress, anxiety, and behavioral issues. It promotes a positive classroom climate where students feel supported and valued.

3. **Positive Relationships**: SEL fosters the development of healthy relationships among students and between students and teachers. It promotes empathy, respect, and effective communication, creating a sense of belonging and community within the classroom.

4. **Conflict Resolution Skills**: SEL equips students with the skills to resolve conflicts peacefully and constructively. It promotes empathy, active listening, and problem-solving, enabling students to navigate disagreements and build positive relationships.

5. **Long-term Success**: The social and emotional skills developed through SEL are not only beneficial during the school years but also have a lasting impact on students' personal and professional lives. SEL prepares students for future challenges, enabling them to thrive in various social and professional contexts.

3.1.4 Implementing SEL in the Classroom

INTEGRATING SEL INTO the classroom requires a deliberate and intentional approach. Educators can incorporate SEL into their teaching practices through various strategies, including:

1. **Explicit Instruction**: Teachers can explicitly teach SEL skills by incorporating lessons and activities that focus on self-awareness, self-management, social awareness, relationship skills, and responsible decision-making.

2. **Modeling**: Educators can model SEL skills by demonstrating empathy, active listening, and positive communication in their interactions with students. By being a role model, teachers can inspire students to develop these skills themselves.

3. **Creating a Supportive Environment**: Teachers can create a safe and inclusive classroom environment where students feel comfortable expressing their emotions and opinions. This can be achieved through establishing clear expectations, promoting respect, and fostering a sense of belonging.

4. **Integration into Academic Subjects**: SEL can be integrated into various academic subjects, allowing students to apply their social and emotional skills in real-world contexts. For example, literature discussions can explore characters' emotions and perspectives, while science experiments can encourage teamwork and problem-solving.

5. **Collaboration with Parents and Community**: Involving parents and the wider community in SEL initiatives can strengthen the impact and reinforce the skills learned in the classroom. Collaborative efforts can include workshops, family engagement activities, and community service projects.

By embracing SEL, educators can create a transformative learning experience that goes beyond academic achievement. It empowers students to become compassionate, resilient, and socially responsible individuals who are equipped to navigate the complexities of life with confidence and empathy. In the following sections, we will delve deeper into each of the core competencies of SEL and explore practical strategies for teaching and fostering these skills in the classroom.

3.2 Teaching Self-Awareness and Self-Management

SELF-AWARENESS AND self-management are essential skills for both teachers and students. By developing these skills, teachers can create a positive and supportive learning environment, while students can learn to understand and regulate their own emotions and behaviors. In this section, we will explore various strategies and techniques to teach self-awareness and self-management effectively.

3.2.1 Cultivating Self-Awareness

SELF-AWARENESS IS THE ability to recognize and understand one's own emotions, thoughts, and behaviors. It is the foundation for developing emotional intelligence and is crucial for personal growth and success. As teachers, we can help our students cultivate self-awareness through various activities and discussions.

Reflective Journaling

ONE EFFECTIVE WAY TO promote self-awareness is through reflective journaling. Encourage students to write about their thoughts, feelings, and experiences on a regular basis. Provide prompts or guiding questions to help them delve deeper into their emotions and gain a better understanding of themselves. By reflecting on their own experiences, students can develop a greater sense of self-awareness.

Mindfulness Practices

INTRODUCING MINDFULNESS practices in the classroom can also enhance self-awareness. Teach students simple mindfulness techniques such as deep breathing exercises, body scans, or guided meditations. These practices can help students become more present in the moment, observe their thoughts and emotions without judgment, and develop a deeper understanding of themselves.

Self-Reflection Activities

ENGAGE STUDENTS IN self-reflection activities that encourage them to think about their strengths, weaknesses, and areas for growth. Provide opportunities for them to assess their own progress and set goals for improvement. By regularly reflecting on their own abilities and progress, students can develop a stronger sense of self-awareness and take ownership of their learning.

3.2.2 Developing Self-Management Skills

SELF-MANAGEMENT REFERS to the ability to regulate one's emotions, thoughts, and behaviors in a positive and productive manner. It involves skills such as impulse control, stress management, and goal-setting. As teachers, we can guide our students in developing these skills through various strategies.

Emotional regulation techniques

TEACH STUDENTS EFFECTIVE techniques for managing their emotions. Encourage them to identify their triggers and develop strategies to cope with difficult emotions. Teach them relaxation techniques such as deep breathing, visualization, or progressive muscle relaxation. By providing students with a toolbox of strategies, they can learn to manage their emotions in a healthy and constructive way.

Goal setting and time management

HELP STUDENTS DEVELOP goal-setting and time-management skills. Teach them how to set SMART (specific, measurable, achievable, relevant, and time-bound) goals and break them down into smaller, manageable tasks. Teach them strategies for prioritizing tasks, managing their time effectively, and staying organized. By developing these skills, students can become more self-directed and better able to manage their responsibilities.

Problem-Solving Skills

ENCOURAGE STUDENTS to develop problem-solving skills by teaching them a structured problem-solving process. Teach them to identify the problem, brainstorm possible solutions, evaluate the pros and cons of each solution, choose the best solution, and implement it. By equipping students with problem-solving skills, they can become more independent and confident in managing challenges that arise.

3.2.3 Integrating Self-Awareness and Self-Management into the Curriculum

TO ENSURE THE DEVELOPMENT of self-awareness and self-management skills, it is important to integrate them into the curriculum across various subjects. Here are some ways to incorporate these skills into different academic areas:

Language Arts

IN THE LANGUAGE ARTS, assign reading materials that explore characters' emotions and motivations. Encourage students to analyze and reflect on the characters' actions and emotions, relating them to their own experiences. This can help students develop empathy and self-awareness.

Social Studies

IN SOCIAL STUDIES, explore historical events and their impact on individuals and societies. Encourage students to reflect on the emotions and motivations of historical figures and analyze how their actions influenced the course of history. This can help students develop a deeper understanding of themselves and others.

Science

IN SCIENCE, TEACH STUDENTS about the physiological and psychological aspects of emotions. Help them understand the connection between emotions and the brain and how emotions can impact overall well-being. This knowledge can empower students to better manage their emotions and make informed decisions.

Mathematics

IN MATHEMATICS, INCORPORATE activities that require students to solve real-life problems and make decisions based on data. This can help students develop critical thinking skills and make connections between their emotions, thoughts, and decision-making processes.

By integrating self-awareness and self-management into the curriculum, we can provide students with opportunities to practice and apply these skills in various contexts, fostering their overall growth and development.

In the next section, we will explore strategies for developing social awareness and relationship skills, which are crucial components of social-emotional learning.

3.3 Developing Social Awareness and Relationship Skills

SOCIAL AWARENESS AND relationship skills are essential components of social-emotional learning (SEL) that contribute to the holistic development of students. By cultivating social awareness, students gain an understanding of themselves and others, develop empathy, and learn to navigate diverse social situations. Relationship skills, on the other hand, enable students to build and maintain healthy relationships, resolve conflicts, and collaborate effectively with their peers. In this section, we will explore various strategies and activities to help teachers foster social awareness and relationship skills in their students.

3.3.1 Cultivating Empathy

EMPATHY IS THE ABILITY to understand and share the feelings of others. It plays a crucial role in developing positive relationships and creating a compassionate classroom environment. As teachers, we can cultivate empathy in our students through various activities and discussions. One effective strategy is to encourage students to put themselves in someone else's shoes by engaging in perspective-taking exercises. For example, students can be asked to imagine how they would feel in a particular situation or to write a letter from the perspective of a character in a story.

Another way to foster empathy is through literature and storytelling. By exposing students to diverse narratives and characters, we can help them develop a deeper understanding of different perspectives and experiences. Reading and discussing books that explore themes of empathy, kindness, and social justice can spark meaningful conversations and inspire students to take action in their own lives.

3.3.2 Building Communication Skills

EFFECTIVE COMMUNICATION is a fundamental aspect of building and maintaining healthy relationships. By teaching students essential communication skills, we empower them to express themselves clearly, listen actively, and resolve conflicts peacefully. One strategy to develop communication skills is through role-playing activities. Students can take on different roles and practice effective communication techniques such as active listening, using "I" statements, and asking clarifying questions.

Collaborative projects and group discussions also provide opportunities for students to practice their communication skills. By working together towards a common goal, students learn to express their ideas, listen to others, and negotiate compromises. Teachers can facilitate these activities by providing clear guidelines for respectful communication and modeling effective communication strategies themselves.

3.3.3 Promoting Diversity and Inclusion

CREATING AN INCLUSIVE classroom environment is essential for fostering social awareness and relationship skills. By celebrating diversity and promoting inclusivity, teachers can help students develop a sense of belonging and respect for others. One way to promote diversity is by incorporating multicultural literature and resources into the curriculum. By exposing students to different cultures, traditions, and perspectives, we can broaden their understanding of the world and promote empathy and acceptance.

Teachers can also create opportunities for students to share their own cultural backgrounds and experiences. This can be done through class presentations, cultural celebrations, or inviting guest speakers from diverse backgrounds. By valuing and respecting each student's unique identity, we create a safe and inclusive space where students feel comfortable expressing themselves and learning from one another.

3.3.4 Nurturing Positive Relationships

BUILDING POSITIVE RELATIONSHIPS between students is crucial for creating a supportive and collaborative classroom community. Teachers can facilitate the development of these relationships by implementing cooperative learning strategies and team-building activities. Group projects, peer tutoring, and collaborative problem-solving tasks provide opportunities for students to work together, learn from each other, and develop trust and respect.

Teachers can also foster positive relationships by modeling positive behavior and providing guidance on conflict resolution. By teaching students effective strategies for resolving conflicts, such as active listening, compromise, and seeking win-win solutions, we empower them to navigate disagreements in a constructive manner. Creating a classroom culture that values open communication, empathy, and respect sets the foundation for strong and positive relationships among students.

3.3.5 Promoting Digital Citizenship

IN TODAY'S DIGITAL age, it is essential to teach students how to navigate the online world responsibly and respectfully. Digital citizenship encompasses the skills and knowledge needed to engage in safe, ethical, and responsible online behavior. By integrating digital citizenship education into the curriculum, teachers can help students develop social awareness and relationship skills in the digital realm.

Teachers can guide students in understanding the importance of online privacy, respectful communication, and responsible use of technology. Discussions on cyberbullying, online etiquette, and critical evaluation of online information can help students develop the necessary skills to navigate the digital world with empathy and integrity. By promoting digital citizenship, teachers empower students to build positive relationships online and contribute to a safe and inclusive digital community.

Incorporating social awareness and relationship skills into the classroom not only enhances students' social-emotional development but also creates a positive and inclusive learning environment. By fostering empathy, communication skills, diversity, positive relationships, and digital citizenship, teachers can equip students with the tools they need to navigate the complexities of the social world and become compassionate and responsible members of society.

3.4 Promoting Responsible Decision-Making

RESPONSIBLE DECISION-making is a crucial skill that students need to develop in order to navigate the complexities of life. It involves considering the consequences of their actions, weighing different options, and making choices that align with their values and goals. As educators, we have the opportunity to guide and support our students in developing this important skill. In this section, we will explore strategies and techniques for promoting responsible decision-making in the classroom.

3.4.1 Creating a Culture of Responsibility

PROMOTING RESPONSIBLE decision-making begins with creating a culture of responsibility in the classroom. This involves setting clear expectations and boundaries and fostering a sense of accountability among students. Here are some strategies to help you create a culture of responsibility:

1. Establish clear rules and consequences: Clearly communicate your expectations to students and establish consequences for not meeting those expectations. Make sure the consequences are fair and consistent.

2. Encourage student involvement in rule-making: Involve students in the process of creating classroom rules. This gives them a sense of ownership and responsibility for their behavior.

3. Model responsible decision-making: Be a role model

for responsible decision-making by demonstrating thoughtful and deliberate decision-making in your own actions and choices.

4. Provide opportunities for reflection. Incorporate reflection activities into your lessons to help students think critically about their decisions and actions. Encourage them to consider the impact of their choices on themselves and others.

3.4.2 Teaching Decision-Making Skills

IN ORDER TO PROMOTE responsible decision-making, it is important to explicitly teach students the skills they need to make informed and thoughtful choices. Here are some strategies for teaching decision-making skills:

1. Introduce decision-making models: Teach students different decision-making models, such as the "STOP" model (Stop, Think, Options, Pick) or the "PRO" model (Problem, Response, Outcome). These models provide a framework for students to follow when making decisions.

2. Provide real-life scenarios: Present students with real-life scenarios and ask them to analyze the situation, consider different options, and make a decision. Encourage them to think about the potential consequences of each option.

3. Role-play decision-making: Engage students in role-playing activities where they can practice making decisions in a safe and supportive environment. This allows them to experience the decision-making

process firsthand and learn from their experiences.

4. Use case studies: Use case studies to explore real-world examples of responsible decision-making. Discuss the choices made by individuals in these scenarios and the impact of those choices.

3.4.3 Developing Critical Thinking Skills

RESPONSIBLE DECISION-making is closely linked to critical thinking skills. By developing students' critical thinking skills, we can empower them to make informed and responsible choices. Here are some strategies for developing critical thinking skills:

1. Encourage questioning: Encourage students to ask questions and challenge assumptions. Teach them to think critically by considering different perspectives and evaluating evidence.

2. Provide opportunities for problem-solving: Present students with open-ended problems or challenges that require them to think critically and come up with creative solutions. This helps them develop their problem-solving and decision-making skills.

3. Foster a growth mindset: Encourage a growth mindset in your classroom, where students believe that their abilities can be developed through effort and practice. This mindset promotes resilience and a willingness to take risks, both of which are important for responsible decision-making.

4. Incorporate critical thinking activities: Integrate critical thinking activities into your lessons, such as

debates, discussions, and analysis of texts or media. These activities encourage students to think critically and make reasoned judgments.

3.4.4 Encouraging Ethical Decision-Making

RESPONSIBLE DECISION-making also involves considering ethical considerations and making choices that align with one's values and principles. Here are some strategies for encouraging ethical decision-making:

1. Discuss ethical dilemmas: Engage students in discussions about ethical dilemmas and ask them to consider different perspectives and possible solutions. Encourage them to think about the ethical implications of their decisions.
2. Teach ethical frameworks: Introduce students to different ethical frameworks, such as utilitarianism, deontology, and virtue ethics. Help them understand how these frameworks can guide their decision-making process.
3. Explore real-world examples: Use real-world examples to illustrate the importance of ethical decision-making. Discuss the consequences of unethical choices and the impact they can have on individuals and society.
4. Promote empathy and compassion: Foster a sense of empathy and compassion in your classroom. Help students understand the impact of their decisions on others and encourage them to consider the well-being of others when making choices.

By promoting responsible decision-making in the classroom, we are equipping our students with the skills and mindset they need to navigate the complexities of life. Through explicit instruction, modeling, and creating a culture of responsibility, we can empower our students to make thoughtful and ethical choices that will positively impact their lives and the lives of others.

3.5 Integrating SEL into Academic Subjects

SOCIAL EMOTIONAL LEARNING (SEL) is a vital component of education that focuses on developing students' emotional intelligence, self-awareness, and interpersonal skills. While SEL is often seen as a separate aspect of education, it can be seamlessly integrated into academic subjects to enhance students' overall learning experience. By incorporating SEL into academic subjects, teachers can create a more holistic and meaningful learning environment for their students.

3.5.1 Benefits of Integrating SEL into Academic Subjects

INTEGRATING SEL INTO academic subjects offers numerous benefits for both students and teachers. When students are taught academic content in conjunction with SEL skills, they are more likely to engage in the learning process and retain information. By connecting academic concepts to real-life situations and emotions, students can develop a deeper understanding of the subject matter.

Furthermore, integrating SEL into academic subjects helps students develop essential life skills such as problem-solving, decision-making, and effective communication. These skills are not only valuable in the classroom but also in their personal and professional lives. By integrating SEL into academic subjects, teachers can equip students with the tools they need to navigate challenges and succeed in various aspects of life.

For teachers, integrating SEL into academic subjects can create a more positive and inclusive classroom environment.

It allows teachers to build stronger relationships with their students and fosters a sense of belonging and trust. Additionally, by incorporating SEL into academic subjects, teachers can address the social and emotional needs of their students, promoting overall well-being and academic success.

3.5.2 Strategies for Integrating SEL into Academic Subjects

INTEGRATING SEL INTO academic subjects requires thoughtful planning and implementation. Here are some strategies that teachers can use to seamlessly incorporate SEL into their lessons:

1. Connect academic content to real-life experiences:

HELP STUDENTS MAKE connections between the academic content they are learning and real-life situations. For example, when teaching a history lesson, discuss the emotions and perspectives of individuals involved in historical events. This helps students develop empathy and a deeper understanding of the subject matter.

2. Use cooperative learning activities:

INCORPORATE COOPERATIVE learning activities that promote teamwork, communication, and collaboration. These activities can be used in any subject area and provide opportunities for students to practice social and emotional skills while working together to achieve a common goal.

3. Teach conflict resolution skills.

INTEGRATE CONFLICT resolution skills into academic subjects by teaching students how to effectively resolve conflicts and manage disagreements. This can be done through role-playing activities, discussions, and problem-solving exercises.

4. Incorporate reflection and self-assessment.

ENCOURAGE STUDENTS to reflect on their learning and emotions by incorporating regular reflection activities into academic subjects. This can be done through journaling, group discussions, or self-assessment tasks. Reflection helps students develop self-awareness and promotes personal growth.

5. Provide opportunities for student voice and choice.

ALLOW STUDENTS TO HAVE a say in their learning by providing opportunities for student voice and choice. This can be done by offering different project options, allowing students to choose topics of interest, or incorporating student-led discussions. By giving students autonomy, they feel more engaged and invested in their learning.

6. Foster a positive classroom culture:

CREATE A POSITIVE CLASSROOM culture that values and celebrates diversity, empathy, and respect. Incorporate activities and discussions that promote inclusivity and understanding. By fostering a positive classroom culture, students feel safe to express themselves and take risks in their learning.

3.5.3 Examples of Integrating SEL into Academic Subjects

HERE ARE SOME EXAMPLES of how SEL can be integrated into different academic subjects:

English Language Arts:

IN AN ENGLISH LANGUAGE Arts class, teachers can incorporate SEL by analyzing characters' emotions and motivations in literature. Students can discuss how characters' actions are influenced by their emotions and reflect on how they can relate to the characters' experiences.

Science:

IN A SCIENCE CLASS, teachers can integrate SEL by exploring the emotional impact of environmental issues. Students can discuss the emotions they feel when learning about climate change or pollution and brainstorm ways to take action and make a positive impact on the environment.

Mathematics:

IN A MATHEMATICS CLASS, teachers can incorporate SEL by using real-life scenarios to solve mathematical problems. Students can work in groups to solve problems related to budgeting, financial planning, or analyzing data. This not only develops their mathematical skills but also their problem-solving and decision-making abilities.

Social Studies:

IN A SOCIAL STUDIES class, teachers can integrate SEL by discussing historical events from different perspectives. Students can explore the emotions and motivations of individuals involved in historical events and analyze the impact of these events on society. This helps students develop empathy and a deeper understanding of historical contexts.

3.5.4 Assessing SEL Integration

ASSESSING THE INTEGRATION of SEL into academic subjects is essential to monitoring students' progress and the effectiveness of the strategies implemented. Teachers can use a variety of assessment methods, including self-assessments, observations, and student reflections. By regularly assessing SEL integration, teachers can make adjustments to their teaching practices and ensure that students are benefiting from the integration of SEL into academic subjects.

Integrating SEL into academic subjects is a powerful way to create a transformative learning experience for students. By connecting academic content to real-life situations and emotions, teachers can help students develop essential social and emotional skills while mastering academic concepts. Through thoughtful planning and implementation, teachers can create a classroom environment that nurtures both academic growth and emotional well-being.

3.6 Assessing and Monitoring SEL Progress

ASSESSING AND MONITORING social emotional learning (SEL) progress is an essential aspect of transformative teaching. It allows educators to gauge the effectiveness of their SEL strategies and interventions, identify areas for improvement, and track the growth and development of their students' social and emotional skills. By regularly assessing and monitoring SEL progress, teachers can ensure that they are providing the necessary support and guidance to help their students thrive both academically and emotionally.

3.6.1 The Importance of Assessment in SEL

ASSESSMENT PLAYS A crucial role in SEL, as it provides valuable insights into students' social and emotional competencies. It helps teachers understand their students' strengths and areas for growth, enabling them to tailor their instruction and interventions accordingly. Assessments also allow educators to measure the impact of their SEL initiatives and make data-informed decisions to enhance their teaching practices.

When assessing SEL, it is important to consider both formative and summative assessments. Formative assessments are ongoing and provide immediate feedback to students, allowing them to reflect on their progress and make necessary adjustments. Summative assessments, on the other hand, are conducted at the end of a unit or period to evaluate overall growth and achievement.

3.6.2 Selecting Appropriate Assessment Tools

CHOOSING THE RIGHT assessment tools is crucial for accurately measuring SEL progress. There are various assessment methods available, each with its own strengths and limitations. It is important for teachers to select tools that align with their instructional goals, are developmentally appropriate for their students, and provide reliable and valid data.

Some commonly used assessment tools for SEL include:

1. Self-Reflection Surveys: These surveys allow students to reflect on their own social and emotional skills, providing valuable insights into their self-awareness and self-management abilities.
2. Observations and Checklists: Teachers can use structured observations and checklists to assess students' social skills, such as their ability to collaborate, communicate effectively, and demonstrate empathy.
3. Rubrics: Rubrics provide clear criteria for assessing specific SEL skills, such as active listening, conflict resolution, or responsible decision-making. They help teachers provide targeted feedback and track progress over time.
4. Performance Tasks: Performance tasks, such as role-plays or group projects, provide opportunities for students to apply their SEL skills in real-life situations. Teachers can assess students' abilities to navigate social interactions, solve problems, and demonstrate empathy through these tasks.
5. Standardized Assessments: Some standardized

assessments, such as the Social Emotional Learning Assessment (SELA) or the Devereux Student Strengths Assessment (DESSA), are specifically designed to measure SEL competencies. These assessments provide a comprehensive overview of students' social and emotional skills and can be used to benchmark progress.

3.6.3 Integrating SEL Assessment into Instruction

TO EFFECTIVELY ASSESS and monitor SEL progress, it is important to integrate assessment practices into daily instruction. This ensures that SEL is not seen as a separate entity but rather as an integral part of the learning process. Here are some strategies for integrating SEL assessment into instruction:

1. Ongoing Reflection: Encourage students to regularly reflect on their social and emotional skills through journaling, self-assessments, or group discussions. This allows them to develop self-awareness and take ownership of their growth.

2. Authentic Assessments: Design assessments that reflect real-life situations and require students to apply their SEL skills. This could include scenarios, case studies, or project-based assessments that assess students' abilities to collaborate, communicate, and problem-solve.

3. Peer and Self-Assessment: Foster a culture of peer and self-assessment where students provide feedback to

their peers and themselves. This promotes collaboration, empathy, and self-reflection.

4. Data Tracking: Use data tracking tools, such as spreadsheets or online platforms, to monitor students' progress over time. This allows for easy visualization of growth and helps identify patterns or areas that require additional support.

5. Student-Led Conferences: Incorporate student-led conferences where students showcase their SEL growth and discuss their strengths and areas for improvement. This promotes self-advocacy and empowers students to take an active role in their own learning.

3.6.4 Collaborating with Colleagues and Families

ASSESSING AND MONITORING SEL progress is not solely the responsibility of the classroom teacher. Collaborating with colleagues and involving families in the assessment process can provide a more holistic view of students' social and emotional development. Here are some ways to collaborate:

1. Professional Learning Communities: Engage in professional learning communities or collaborative teams to share assessment strategies, discuss student progress, and learn from one another's experiences.

2. Interdisciplinary Collaboration: Collaborate with colleagues from different subject areas to integrate SEL assessment into various academic disciplines.

This promotes a comprehensive approach to SEL and reinforces its importance across the curriculum.

3. Family Engagement: Involve families in the assessment process by sharing assessment results, discussing growth areas, and providing resources for supporting SEL at home. This partnership between home and school enhances the continuity of SEL development.

By assessing and monitoring SEL progress, educators can ensure that their teaching practices are effectively promoting students' social and emotional growth. It allows for targeted interventions, personalized instruction, and the creation of a supportive and nurturing learning environment. Through ongoing assessment, teachers can empower their students to develop the necessary skills to thrive academically, emotionally, and socially.

Chapter 4 : Tending the Teacher's Garden

3.6 Assessing and Monitoring SEL Progress

Assessing and monitoring social emotional learning (SEL) progress is an essential aspect of transformative teaching. It allows educators to gauge the effectiveness of their SEL strategies and interventions, identify areas for improvement, and track the growth and development of their students' social and emotional skills. By regularly assessing and monitoring SEL progress, teachers can ensure that they are providing the necessary support and guidance to help their students thrive both academically and emotionally.

3.6.1 The Importance of Assessment in SEL

ASSESSMENT PLAYS A crucial role in SEL, as it provides valuable insights into students' social and emotional competencies. It helps teachers understand their students' strengths and areas for growth, enabling them to tailor their instruction and interventions accordingly. Assessments also allow educators to measure the impact of their SEL initiatives and make data-informed decisions to enhance their teaching practices.

When assessing SEL, it is important to consider both formative and summative assessments. Formative assessments are ongoing and provide immediate feedback to students, allowing them to reflect on their progress and make necessary adjustments. Summative assessments, on the other hand, are conducted at the end of a unit or period to evaluate overall growth and achievement.

3.6.2 Selecting Appropriate Assessment Tools

CHOOSING THE RIGHT assessment tools is crucial for accurately measuring SEL progress. There are various assessment methods available, each with its own strengths and limitations. It is important for teachers to select tools that align with their instructional goals, are developmentally appropriate for their students, and provide reliable and valid data.

Some commonly used assessment tools for SEL include:

1. Self-Reflection Surveys: These surveys allow students to reflect on their own social and emotional skills, providing valuable insights into their self-awareness and self-management abilities.

2. Observations and Checklists: Teachers can use structured observations and checklists to assess students' social skills, such as their ability to collaborate, communicate effectively, and demonstrate empathy.

3. Rubrics: Rubrics provide clear criteria for assessing specific SEL skills, such as active listening, conflict resolution, or responsible decision-making. They help teachers provide targeted feedback and track progress

over time.

4. Performance Tasks: Performance tasks, such as role-plays or group projects, provide opportunities for students to apply their SEL skills in real-life situations. Teachers can assess students' abilities to navigate social interactions, solve problems, and demonstrate empathy through these tasks.

5. Standardized Assessments: Some standardized assessments, such as the Social Emotional Learning Assessment (SELA) or the Devereux Student Strengths Assessment (DESSA), are specifically designed to measure SEL competencies. These assessments provide a comprehensive overview of students' social and emotional skills and can be used to benchmark progress.

4.1 Self-Care for Teachers

TEACHING IS A NOBLE profession that requires immense dedication, passion, and energy. As educators, we pour our hearts and souls into our work, striving to make a positive impact on the lives of our students. However, in the midst of our commitment to others, it is crucial that we also prioritize our own well-being. Self-care for teachers is not a luxury; it is a necessity. Just as we tend to the needs of our students, we must also tend to our own needs in order to maintain our physical, mental, and emotional health.

4.1.1 The Importance of Self-Care

TEACHING CAN BE A DEMANDING and stressful profession. From managing classrooms to planning lessons, grading assignments, and dealing with various challenges, teachers often find themselves overwhelmed and exhausted. Neglecting self-care can lead to burnout, decreased job satisfaction, and even physical and mental health issues. It is essential for teachers to recognize that taking care of themselves is not selfish but rather a vital aspect of being an effective educator.

4.1.2 Prioritizing Physical Health

PHYSICAL WELL-BEING is the foundation of self-care. As teachers, we must prioritize our physical health to ensure that we have the energy and stamina to meet the demands of our profession. This includes getting enough sleep, eating nutritious meals, and engaging in regular exercise. Adequate rest, a balanced diet, and physical activity not only contribute to our overall health but also enhance our ability to manage stress and maintain a positive mindset.

4.1.3 Nurturing Mental and Emotional Well-Being

TEACHING CAN BE EMOTIONALLY challenging as we navigate the highs and lows of our students' experiences and emotions. It is crucial for teachers to develop strategies to nurture their own mental and emotional well-being. This may involve practicing mindfulness and relaxation techniques, seeking support from colleagues or mentors, and engaging in activities that bring joy and fulfillment outside of the classroom. Taking time for hobbies, spending time with loved ones, and pursuing personal interests can help us recharge and maintain a healthy work-life balance.

4.1.4 Setting Boundaries

ONE OF THE GREATEST challenges for teachers is finding a balance between their professional and personal lives. It is important to establish clear boundaries to prevent work from consuming every aspect of our lives. This may involve setting limits on work hours, creating designated time for self-care activities, and learning to say no when necessary. By setting boundaries, we can protect our well-being and ensure that we have the time and energy to devote to ourselves and our loved ones.

4.1.5 Seeking Support and Professional Development

TEACHERS SHOULD NEVER underestimate the power of support and professional development. Connecting with colleagues, participating in professional learning communities, and seeking guidance from mentors can provide valuable insights, encouragement, and a sense of belonging. Additionally, attending workshops, conferences, and continuing education courses can enhance our teaching skills and keep us inspired and motivated. By investing in our own growth and development, we not only improve our teaching practice but also demonstrate the importance of lifelong learning to our students.

4.1.6 Practicing Self-Reflection

SELF-REFLECTION IS a powerful tool for personal growth and self-care. Taking the time to reflect on our teaching practice, our successes, and our challenges allows us to gain valuable insights and make necessary adjustments. By regularly evaluating our teaching methods, classroom management strategies, and overall well-being, we can identify areas for improvement and implement changes that will benefit both ourselves and our students. Self-reflection also helps us celebrate our achievements and acknowledge the positive impact we have on the lives of our students.

4.1.7 Cultivating a Supportive Teacher Community

BUILDING A SUPPORTIVE teacher community is essential for self-care. Surrounding ourselves with like-minded educators who understand the joys and challenges of teaching can provide a sense of camaraderie and support. Collaborating with colleagues, sharing ideas and resources, and engaging in professional conversations can help alleviate feelings of isolation and promote a positive and nurturing work environment. By fostering a supportive teacher community, we create a space where we can lean on one another, share experiences, and grow together.

4.1.8 Embracing Self-Care as a Lifelong Practice

SELF-CARE IS NOT A one-time event but rather a lifelong practice. As educators, we must commit to prioritizing our own well-being throughout our careers. By consistently engaging in self-care activities, seeking support, and nurturing our physical, mental, and emotional health, we can sustain our passion for teaching and continue to make a positive impact on the lives of our students. Remember, taking care of ourselves is not only beneficial for us but also for those we serve.

In the next section, we will explore strategies for managing stress and burnout, which are common challenges faced by teachers.

3.6.3 Integrating SEL Assessment into Instruction

TO EFFECTIVELY ASSESS and monitor SEL progress, it is important to integrate assessment practices into daily instruction. This ensures that SEL is not seen as a separate entity but rather as an integral part of the learning process. Here are some strategies for integrating SEL assessment into instruction:

1. Ongoing Reflection: Encourage students to regularly reflect on their social and emotional skills through journaling, self-assessments, or group discussions. This allows them to develop self-awareness and take ownership of their growth.

2. Authentic Assessments: Design assessments that reflect real-life situations and require students to apply their SEL skills. This could include scenarios, case studies, or project-based assessments that assess students' abilities to collaborate, communicate, and problem-solve.

3. Peer and Self-Assessment: Foster a culture of peer and

self-assessment where students provide feedback to their peers and themselves. This promotes collaboration, empathy, and self-reflection.

4. Data Tracking: Use data tracking tools, such as spreadsheets or online platforms, to monitor students' progress over time. This allows for easy visualization of growth and helps identify patterns or areas that require additional support.

5. Student-Led Conferences: Incorporate student-led conferences where students showcase their SEL growth and discuss their strengths and areas for improvement. This promotes self-advocacy and empowers students to take an active role in their own learning.

3.6.4 Collaborating with Colleagues and Families

ASSESSING AND MONITORING SEL progress is not solely the responsibility of the classroom teacher. Collaborating with colleagues and involving families in the assessment process can provide a more holistic view of students' social and emotional development. Here are some ways to collaborate:

1. Professional Learning Communities: Engage in professional learning communities or collaborative teams to share assessment strategies, discuss student progress, and learn from one another's experiences.

2. Interdisciplinary Collaboration: Collaborate with colleagues from different subject areas to integrate

SEL assessment into various academic disciplines. This promotes a comprehensive approach to SEL and reinforces its importance across the curriculum.

3. Family Engagement: Involve families in the assessment process by sharing assessment results, discussing growth areas, and providing resources for supporting SEL at home. This partnership between home and school enhances the continuity of SEL development.

By assessing and monitoring SEL progress, educators can ensure that their teaching practices are effectively promoting students' social and emotional growth. It allows for targeted interventions, personalized instruction, and the creation of a supportive and nurturing learning environment. Through ongoing assessment, teachers can empower their students to develop the necessary skills to thrive academically, emotionally, and socially.

4.2 Managing Stress and Burnout

TEACHING IS A REWARDING profession that allows educators to make a positive impact on the lives of their students. However, it can also be a demanding and stressful job. The constant pressure to meet academic standards, manage classroom dynamics, and juggle administrative tasks can take a toll on teachers' well-being. It is essential for educators to prioritize their mental and emotional health to avoid burnout and maintain their passion for teaching. In this section, we will explore strategies for managing stress and preventing burnout in the teaching profession.

4.2.1 Recognizing the Signs of Stress and Burnout

STRESS AND BURNOUT can manifest in various ways, and it is crucial for teachers to be aware of the signs and symptoms. Some common indicators of stress and burnout include the following:

1. Physical symptoms such as fatigue, headaches, and frequent illnesses.
2. Emotional exhaustion and a sense of being overwhelmed
3. Increased irritability and impatience.
4. Loss of motivation and a decline in job satisfaction.
5. Difficulty concentrating and making decisions.
6. Withdrawal from social activities and a decrease in personal relationships.

By recognizing these signs, teachers can take proactive steps to address their stress levels and prevent burnout.

4.2.2 Self-Care Practices for Teachers

SELF-CARE IS ESSENTIAL for teachers to maintain their well-being and prevent burnout. Here are some self-care practices that educators can incorporate into their daily lives:

1. Prioritize personal time: Set aside time each day for activities that bring you joy and relaxation. Whether it's reading a book, practicing yoga, or taking a walk in nature, make sure to carve out time for yourself.
2. Establish boundaries: It's important to set boundaries between work and personal life. Avoid bringing work home whenever possible, and create a schedule that allows for downtime and relaxation.
3. Practice mindfulness and meditation. Engaging in mindfulness exercises and meditation can help reduce stress and promote a sense of calm. Take a few minutes each day to focus on your breath and be present in the moment.
4. Engage in physical activity: Regular exercise has numerous benefits for both physical and mental health. Find an activity that you enjoy, whether it's going for a run, attending a yoga class, or playing a sport.
5. Connect with others: Building a support network of colleagues, friends, and family members can provide a valuable outlet for sharing experiences and seeking support. Make time for social connections and engage

in activities that foster positive relationships.

4.2.3 Stress Management Techniques

IN ADDITION TO SELF-care practices, there are various stress management techniques that teachers can utilize to reduce stress levels and promote well-being. Here are a few effective strategies:

1. Time management: Develop effective time management skills to prioritize tasks and avoid feeling overwhelmed. Break larger tasks into smaller, manageable steps and create a schedule or to-do list to stay organized.
2. Seek support: Don't hesitate to reach out for support when needed. Whether it's talking to a trusted colleague, seeking guidance from a mentor, or accessing counseling services, having someone to talk to can provide valuable perspective and support.
3. Practice relaxation techniques: Incorporate relaxation techniques into your daily routine to reduce stress. Deep breathing exercises, progressive muscle relaxation, and guided imagery can help promote relaxation and reduce anxiety.
4. Engage in hobbies and interests: Pursuing hobbies and interests outside of teaching can provide a much-needed break and help alleviate stress. Whether it's painting, playing a musical instrument, or gardening, find activities that bring you joy and allow you to recharge.
5. Reflect and journal: Take time to reflect on your

teaching experiences and journal about your thoughts and feelings. Writing can be a therapeutic outlet and help you gain insights into your emotions and stress triggers.

4.2.4 Seeking Professional Development and Support

CONTINUAL PROFESSIONAL development is crucial for teachers to stay motivated and engaged in their profession. Seek out opportunities for growth and learning, whether it's attending conferences, participating in workshops, or pursuing advanced degrees. Engaging in professional development can provide new perspectives, enhance teaching skills, and prevent stagnation.

Additionally, building a supportive teacher community can be invaluable in managing stress and preventing burnout. Connect with fellow educators through professional organizations, online forums, or local teacher groups. Sharing experiences, seeking advice, and collaborating with others can provide a sense of camaraderie and support.

Remember, managing stress and preventing burnout is an ongoing process. It requires self-awareness, self-care, and a commitment to prioritizing your well-being. By implementing these strategies and seeking support when needed, teachers can cultivate a healthy work-life balance and continue to thrive in their profession.

4.3 Professional Development and

Growth

AS A TEACHER, YOUR journey of growth and development is never-ending. Just as you strive to nurture the minds and hearts of your students, it is equally important to tend to your own growth as an educator. Professional development plays a vital role in enhancing your teaching skills, expanding your knowledge, and staying up-to-date with the latest educational practices. In this section, we will explore the importance of professional development and provide strategies for your ongoing growth.

4.3.1 The Value of Professional Development

PROFESSIONAL DEVELOPMENT is not just a requirement for maintaining your teaching certification; it is an opportunity for personal and professional growth. Engaging in continuous learning and development allows you to stay current with educational trends, research, and best practices. It enables you to refine your teaching strategies, enhance your instructional techniques, and adapt to the evolving needs of your students.

By investing in your own professional development, you are also investing in the success of your students. As you acquire new knowledge and skills, you can bring innovative and effective teaching methods into your classroom. Professional development also provides a platform for collaboration and networking with other educators, allowing you to learn from their experiences and share your own insights.

4.3.2 Setting Professional Goals

TO MAKE THE MOST OF your professional development opportunities, it is essential to set clear goals. Reflect on your teaching practice and identify areas where you would like to grow and improve. Consider the needs of your students, the challenges you face in the classroom, and the areas of teaching that you are passionate about. Use these reflections to set specific, measurable, achievable, relevant, and time-bound (SMART) goals.

For example, your professional goals might include improving your classroom management skills, incorporating more technology into your lessons, or deepening your understanding of a specific subject area. By setting goals, you can focus your professional development efforts and ensure that you are investing your time and energy in areas that will have the greatest impact on your teaching practice.

4.3.3 Professional Development Opportunities

THERE ARE NUMEROUS avenues for professional development that can support your growth as an educator. Here are some common opportunities to consider:

4.3.3.1 Workshops and Conferences

ATTENDING WORKSHOPS and conferences allows you to learn from experts in the field and gain insights into the latest research and practices. These events often provide a range of sessions and workshops tailored to different subject areas and teaching levels. Take advantage of these opportunities to expand your knowledge, network with other educators, and discover new teaching strategies.

4.3.3.2 Online Courses and Webinars

ONLINE COURSES AND webinars offer flexibility and convenience, allowing you to engage in professional development from the comfort of your own home. Many reputable organizations and educational institutions offer online courses on a wide range of topics, from pedagogy to technology integration. These courses often provide interactive modules, discussion forums, and assessments to ensure a comprehensive learning experience.

4.3.3.3 Professional Learning Communities

JOINING A PROFESSIONAL learning community (PLC) provides a supportive network of educators who share a common interest or focus area. PLCs can be formed within your school, district, or online platforms. Engaging in regular discussions, sharing resources, and collaborating with other educators can greatly enhance your professional growth. Consider joining a PLC that aligns with your goals and interests to foster ongoing learning and collaboration.

4.3.3.4 Mentoring and Coaching

SEEKING OUT A MENTOR or coach can provide personalized guidance and support in your professional development journey. A mentor, who is an experienced educator, can offer valuable insights, advice, and feedback based on their own experiences. A coach, on the other hand, can work with you to set goals, develop action plans, and provide ongoing support and accountability. Both mentoring and coaching relationships can be instrumental in your growth as a teacher.

4.3.3.5 Reflective Practice

ENGAGING IN REFLECTIVE practice is a powerful tool for professional development. Take time to reflect on your teaching practice, analyze your successes and challenges, and identify areas for improvement. Consider keeping a reflective journal or participating in reflective discussions with colleagues. Reflective practice allows you to gain a deeper understanding of your teaching methods, make informed decisions, and continuously refine your practice.

4.3.4 Implementing Professional Development

TO MAKE THE MOST OF your professional development opportunities, it is important to approach them with intention and purpose. Here are some strategies to help you implement your professional development effectively:

4.3.4.1 Create a Professional Development Plan

DEVELOP A PLAN THAT outlines your professional goals, the specific activities you will engage in, and a timeline for completion. This plan will serve as a roadmap for your professional development journey and help you stay focused and organized.

4.3.4.2 Seek feedback and reflect.

REGULARLY SEEK FEEDBACK from your colleagues, administrators, and students. Reflect on this feedback and use it to inform your professional development goals and actions. Embrace a growth mindset and view feedback as an opportunity for improvement.

4.3.4.3 Collaborate with colleagues.

ENGAGE IN COLLABORATIVE learning with your colleagues. Share resources, exchange ideas, and discuss best practices. Collaborating with others can provide fresh perspectives and inspire new approaches to teaching.

4.3.4.4 Apply new knowledge and skills.

AS YOU ENGAGE IN PROFESSIONAL development activities, actively seek opportunities to apply what you have learned in your classroom. Experiment with new strategies, techniques, and technologies. Reflect on the outcomes and make adjustments as needed.

4.3.4.5 Reflect and revise

REGULARLY REFLECT ON your professional development journey. Assess the impact of your efforts on your teaching practice and student learning. Revise your goals and action plans as necessary to ensure ongoing growth and improvement.

Remember, professional development is not a one-time event but a continuous process. Embrace the opportunity to grow as an educator, and let your passion for learning inspire your students to do the same.

4.4 Building a Supportive Teacher Community

TEACHING CAN OFTEN be a solitary profession, with educators spending most of their time in their classrooms, focused on their students. However, building a supportive teacher community is essential for personal and professional growth. A strong network of colleagues can provide emotional support, share ideas and resources, and offer a sense of belonging in a profession that can sometimes feel isolating. In this section, we will explore the importance of building a supportive teacher community and provide practical strategies for doing so.

4.4.1 The Power of Collaboration

COLLABORATION AMONG teachers is a powerful tool for professional development and growth. When teachers come together to share their experiences, expertise, and ideas, they can learn from one another and enhance their teaching practices. Collaborative environments foster creativity, innovation, and a sense of camaraderie among educators.

One way to foster collaboration is through professional learning communities (PLCs). PLCs are groups of teachers who meet regularly to discuss teaching strategies, share resources, and reflect on their practice. These communities provide a safe space for teachers to ask questions, seek advice, and receive feedback from their peers. PLCs can be formed within a school or across different schools, and they can focus on specific subjects, grade levels, or teaching methodologies.

Another way to encourage collaboration is through mentorship programs. Experienced teachers can serve as mentors to new or less experienced teachers, providing guidance, support, and encouragement. Mentorship programs create opportunities for teachers to learn from one another, develop new skills, and build lasting relationships.

4.4.2 Professional Learning Networks

IN ADDITION TO COLLABORATING within their own school community, teachers can also expand their professional networks by connecting with educators outside of their immediate environment. Professional learning networks (PLNs) provide opportunities for teachers to connect with colleagues from around the world, share ideas, and engage in meaningful discussions.

Social media platforms, such as Twitter and Facebook, have become popular spaces for educators to connect and collaborate. Teachers can join online communities, participate in Twitter chats, and follow education-related hashtags to stay updated on the latest trends and research in the field. These online networks allow teachers to access a wealth of knowledge and resources, and they provide a platform for sharing successes and challenges.

Attending conferences, workshops, and seminars is another way for teachers to expand their professional networks. These events bring together educators from different schools and districts, providing opportunities for networking, learning, and professional growth. Teachers can attend sessions, participate in panel discussions, and engage in conversations with like-minded professionals. Conferences also offer a chance to discover new teaching strategies, technologies, and resources that can enhance classroom instruction.

4.4.3 Cultivating Relationships

BUILDING A SUPPORTIVE teacher community is not just about professional collaboration; it is also about cultivating meaningful relationships with colleagues. Taking the time to get to know fellow teachers on a personal level can create a sense of belonging and foster a positive work environment.

One way to cultivate relationships is through informal gatherings, such as teacher lunches or after-school social events. These casual settings provide opportunities for teachers to connect, share stories, and build friendships. By creating a relaxed and welcoming atmosphere, teachers can develop a sense of camaraderie and support.

Collaborative projects and team-teaching opportunities also promote relationship-building among teachers. Working together on a shared goal or project allows teachers to learn from one another, leverage each other's strengths, and develop a sense of trust and respect. Collaborative projects can range from co-planning lessons to organizing school-wide events, providing opportunities for teachers to collaborate and build relationships outside of their own classrooms.

4.4.4 Supporting Teacher Well-Being

A SUPPORTIVE TEACHER community should also prioritize the well-being of its members. Teaching can be a demanding and stressful profession, and having a network of colleagues who understand and empathize with these challenges can make a significant difference.

Creating spaces for self-care and well-being within the teacher community is essential. This can include organizing wellness activities, such as yoga or meditation sessions, providing access to resources on stress management and self-care, and encouraging open conversations about mental health. By prioritizing well-being, teachers can support one another in maintaining a healthy work-life balance and preventing burnout.

Additionally, recognizing and celebrating the achievements and contributions of teachers within the community is crucial. Acknowledging the hard work and dedication of colleagues can boost morale and create a positive and supportive atmosphere. This can be done through staff appreciation events, awards, or simply taking the time to express gratitude and appreciation for one another's efforts.

In conclusion, building a supportive teacher community is essential for personal and professional growth. Collaboration, professional learning networks, cultivating relationships, and supporting teacher well-being are all key components of a strong teacher community. By investing in these areas, educators can create a network of support, share ideas and resources, and foster a positive and enriching work environment.

Chapter 5: The Gallery of Activities

5.1 Engaging Icebreaker Activities

I cebreaker activities are a fantastic way to start a class or workshop on a positive note. They help create a welcoming and inclusive environment, allowing participants to get to know each other and feel more comfortable expressing themselves. These activities can also serve as a bridge between the teacher and students, fostering a sense of connection and trust. In this section, we will explore a variety of engaging icebreaker activities that can be used in different educational settings.

5.1.1 Two Truths and a Lie

TWO TRUTHS AND A LIE is a classic icebreaker activity that encourages participants to share interesting facts about themselves while also challenging others to identify the false statement. To play this game, each participant takes turns sharing three statements about themselves, two of which are true and one that is false. The rest of the group then tries to guess which statement is a lie. This activity not only helps break the ice but also encourages active listening and critical thinking.

5.1.2 Human Bingo

HUMAN BINGO IS A FUN and interactive icebreaker activity that encourages participants to interact with each other and find commonalities. Create a bingo grid with different statements or characteristics in each square, such as "Has traveled to another country" or "Plays a musical instrument." Participants then mingle and try to find someone who matches each statement. Once they find a match, they can have that person sign the corresponding square. The goal is to fill the entire bingo grid as quickly as possible. This activity promotes communication, collaboration, and the discovery of shared interests.

5.1.3 Name That Emoji

NAME THAT EMOJI IS a creative icebreaker activity that combines technology and emotions. Create a list of different emojis and their corresponding emotions, such as ☺ (happy), ☹ (sad), or ☹ (angr). Show each emoji to tparticipantsts, and ask them to guess the corresponding emotion. Encourage them to share why they think a particular emoji represents a specific emotion. This activity not only helps participants become more familiar with different emotions but also sparks discussions about the complexities of human emotions.

5.1.4 Desert Island

DESERT ISLAND IS A thought-provoking icebreaker activity that encourages participants to think critically and creatively. Ask each participant to imagine they are stranded on a desert island and can only bring three items with them. They must then share their three chosen items and explain why they are essential for their survival or well-being. This activity not only helps participants get to know each other on a deeper level but also encourages them to think outside the box and consider the value of different objects.

5.1.5 Picture Perfect

PICTURE PERFECT IS a visual icebreaker activity that encourages participants to share their perspectives and interpretations. Provide each participant with a picture or photograph and ask them to describe what they see, how it makes them feel, and what story it tells. Participants can then share their thoughts with the rest of the group. This activity promotes creativity, observation skills, and empathy as participants learn to appreciate different perspectives and interpretations.

5.1.6 Would You Rather?

WOULD YOU RATHER? IS a lighthearted icebreaker activity that presents participants with two hypothetical scenarios and asks them to choose which option they prefer. For example, "Would you rather have the ability to fly or be invisible?" Participants take turns sharing their choices and explaining their reasoning. This activity not only sparks interesting discussions but also helps participants understand each other's preferences and values.

5.1.7 Group Jigsaw Puzzle

GROUP JIGSAW PUZZLE is a collaborative icebreaker activity that requires participants to work together to solve a puzzle. Divide the class into small groups, and provide each group with a jigsaw puzzle. Instruct them to work together to complete the puzzle as quickly as possible. This activity promotes teamwork, communication, and problem-solving skills. It also helps participants develop patience and learn the importance of collaboration.

5.1.8 Speed Networking

SPEED NETWORKING IS an energetic icebreaker activity that allows participants to meet and interact with multiple people in a short amount of time. Set up two rows of chairs facing each other, with participants sitting across from each other. Give them a specific amount of time (e.g., one minute) to introduce themselves, share something interesting about themselves, and ask a question. When the time is up, one row of participants moves to the next chair, and the process repeats. This activity promotes quick thinking, active listening, and networking skills.

These engaging icebreaker activities are just a few examples of how you can create a positive and inclusive learning environment. Remember to choose activities that align with the age and interests of your students, and always be mindful of any potential sensitivities or cultural differences. Icebreakers are a powerful tool for building connections and setting the stage for transformative teaching.

5.2 Creative and Expressive Arts in Teaching

ART HAS THE POWER TO transcend language barriers, ignite imagination, and foster self-expression. Incorporating creative and expressive arts into teaching can be a transformative experience for both teachers and students. This section explores the various ways in which educators can utilize art forms such as visual arts, music, drama, and dance to enhance the learning process and create a dynamic and engaging classroom environment.

5.2.1 The Power of Visual Arts

THE VISUAL ARTS ENCOMPASS a wide range of mediums, including drawing, painting, sculpture, and photography. Integrating visual arts into teaching allows students to explore their creativity, develop critical thinking skills, and express their emotions. Here are some strategies for incorporating visual arts in the classroom:

1. **Artistic Reflections**: Encourage students to create visual representations of their learning experiences. For example, after reading a novel, students can create a collage that represents the themes and characters in the story. This activity not only reinforces comprehension but also allows students to engage with the material on a deeper level.

2. **Art Appreciation**: Introduce students to different art styles and artists. Take them on virtual or physical field trips to art museums or galleries. Discuss the techniques used by artists and encourage students to analyze and interpret the artwork. This

not only enhances their understanding of art but also promotes critical thinking and cultural appreciation.

3. **Art Integration**: Integrate visual arts into other academic subjects. For example, in a science class, students can create models or diagrams to represent scientific concepts. In history, they can create timelines or historical portraits. This interdisciplinary approach not only reinforces learning but also allows students to explore different ways of expressing their understanding.

5.2.2 The Melody of Music

MUSIC HAS A UNIQUE ability to evoke emotions, enhance memory, and promote creativity. Incorporating music into teaching can create a vibrant and engaging learning environment. Here are some ways to incorporate music in the classroom:

1. **Background Music**: Play soft instrumental music during independent work or group activities. This can help create a calm and focused atmosphere, enhance concentration, and reduce stress.

2. **Musical Mnemonics**: Use catchy tunes or songs to help students remember important information. For example, creating a song to remember the multiplication tables or a rap to remember the parts of speech can make learning more enjoyable and memorable.

3. **Musical Interpretation**: Select songs that relate to the themes or topics being studied and encourage students to analyze the lyrics and discuss the emotions conveyed. This can deepen their understanding of the material and promote critical thinking.

4. **Musical Performances**: Organize musical performances or invite musicians to the classroom. This can expose students to different genres of music, inspire creativity, and provide opportunities for cultural exchange.

5.2.3 The Magic of Drama

DRAMA ALLOWS STUDENTS to step into different roles, explore different perspectives, and develop empathy. It also enhances communication skills, creativity, and problem-solving abilities. Here are some ways to incorporate drama in the classroom:

1. **Role-playing**: Assign students different roles or characters from a story or historical event and have them act out scenes. This helps bring the material to life and allows students to develop a deeper understanding of the characters and their motivations.

2. **Improvisation**: Engage students in improvisational activities where they have to think on their feet and respond to different scenarios. This promotes quick thinking, creativity, and teamwork.

3. **Reader's Theater**: Have students perform scripts or plays based on literature they have read. This not only enhances their comprehension but also develops their public speaking and presentation skills.

4. **Drama as a Teaching Tool**: Use drama techniques such as freeze frames, hot seating, or thought-tracking to explore complex topics or facilitate discussions. This allows students to engage with the material in a more interactive and meaningful way.

5.2.4 The Rhythm of Dance

DANCE IS A POWERFUL form of self-expression that combines movement, rhythm, and emotion. It promotes physical fitness, coordination, and self-confidence. Here are some ways to incorporate dance in the classroom:

1. **Movement Breaks**: Incorporate short dance or movement breaks during long periods of sitting or intense cognitive activities. This helps energize students, improve focus, and release tension.

2. **Cultural Dance Exploration**: Introduce students to different cultural dances from around the world. Teach them basic steps and movements, and encourage them to create their own dance routines inspired by different cultures. This promotes cultural appreciation and creativity.

3. **Dance as a Storytelling Tool**: Have students create dance routines that tell a story or convey a message. This allows them to combine their creativity with their understanding of a particular topic or theme.

4. **Dance Collaboration**: Organize dance collaborations with other classrooms or schools. This provides opportunities for students to work together, learn from each other, and celebrate diversity.

Incorporating creative and expressive arts in teaching not only enhances the learning experience but also nurtures students' emotional well-being, creativity, and self-confidence. By embracing the power of art, teachers can create a classroom environment that inspires and empowers students to reach their full potential.

5.3 Collaborative Learning Strategies

COLLABORATIVE LEARNING is a powerful approach that encourages students to work together, share ideas, and learn from one another. It promotes active engagement, critical thinking, and problem-solving skills. By fostering a sense of community and cooperation in the classroom, collaborative learning strategies create an environment where students can thrive and grow both academically and socially.

5.3.1 Group Projects

GROUP PROJECTS ARE a popular collaborative learning strategy that allows students to work together towards a common goal. These projects can take various forms, such as research assignments, presentations, or creative tasks. By working in groups, students have the opportunity to share their knowledge, skills, and perspectives, which leads to a deeper understanding of the subject matter. It also helps develop important skills like communication, teamwork, and leadership.

To ensure the success of group projects, it is essential to provide clear guidelines and expectations. Assign roles and responsibilities to each group member, and encourage them to collaborate and support one another. Regular check-ins and progress updates can help keep the project on track and allow for any necessary adjustments. Additionally, providing opportunities for self-reflection and peer evaluation can help students assess their own contributions and learn from the experience.

5.3.2 Think-Pair-Share

THINK-PAIR-SHARE IS a simple yet effective collaborative learning strategy that promotes active participation and critical thinking. It involves three stages: thinking individually, discussing with a partner, and sharing with the whole class. This strategy encourages students to reflect on a question or problem individually, then share their thoughts with a partner before presenting their ideas to the larger group.

To implement Think-Pair-Share, start by posing a thought-provoking question or presenting a challenging problem to the class. Give students a few moments to think silently and jot down their ideas. Next, ask them to pair up with a partner and share their thoughts. Encourage active listening and respectful discussion. Finally, invite a few pairs to share their ideas with the whole class, fostering a collaborative learning environment where everyone's voices are heard.

5.3.3 Jigsaw Technique

THE JIGSAW TECHNIQUE is a cooperative learning strategy that promotes interdependence and active engagement. It involves dividing a complex topic or task into smaller parts and assigning each part to a different group. Each group becomes an expert on their assigned part and then shares their knowledge with the rest of the class.

To implement the jigsaw technique, divide the class into small groups and assign each group a specific subtopic or aspect of the larger topic. Provide resources and materials for each group to research and become experts on their assigned part. After a designated period of time, regroup the students so that each new group has at least one member who is an expert on each subtopic. In these new groups, students take turns sharing their expertise and learning from one another. This collaborative approach encourages active participation, deep understanding, and a sense of shared responsibility.

5.3.4 Peer Tutoring

PEER TUTORING IS A collaborative learning strategy that involves pairing students of different skill levels to work together. The more advanced student acts as a tutor, providing guidance and support to the less advanced student. This approach benefits both the tutor and the tutee, as it reinforces the tutor's knowledge and helps the tutee gain a deeper understanding of the subject matter.

To implement peer tutoring, carefully select pairs based on the students' abilities and needs. Provide clear guidelines and expectations for the tutoring sessions, and encourage open communication and mutual respect. The tutor can explain concepts, answer questions, and provide examples, while the tutee can actively engage in the learning process and seek clarification when needed. Peer tutoring not only enhances academic performance but also promotes empathy, patience, and a sense of community in the classroom.

5.3.5 Collaborative Problem-Solving

COLLABORATIVE PROBLEM-solving is a dynamic learning strategy that encourages students to work together to find solutions to complex problems or challenges. It promotes critical thinking, creativity, and effective communication skills.

By engaging in collaborative problem-solving activities, students learn to approach problems from different perspectives, consider multiple solutions, and negotiate and compromise with their peers.

To implement collaborative problem-solving, present students with a real-world problem or challenge that requires critical thinking and creativity. Divide them into small groups and encourage them to brainstorm ideas, analyze the problem, and propose possible solutions. Facilitate discussions and encourage active participation from all group members. Finally, have each group present their solutions and engage in a class-wide discussion to compare and evaluate different approaches. Collaborative problem-solving not only enhances students' problem-solving skills but also fosters teamwork, resilience, and adaptability.

Collaborative learning strategies provide students with valuable opportunities to learn from one another, develop important social skills, and deepen their understanding of the subject matter. By incorporating these strategies into your teaching practice, you can create a collaborative and inclusive classroom environment that nurtures the growth and success of all students.

5.4 Incorporating Technology for Interactive Learning

IN TODAY'S DIGITAL age, technology has become an integral part of our lives, including in the field of education. Incorporating technology into the classroom can enhance the learning experience and provide students with interactive and engaging opportunities. In this section, we will explore various ways teachers can use technology to create an interactive learning environment.

5.4.1 Interactive Presentations and Multimedia Tools

ONE OF THE MOST COMMON ways to incorporate technology into teaching is through interactive presentations and multimedia tools. Platforms such as PowerPoint, Prezi, and Google Slides allow teachers to create visually appealing presentations that can include images, videos, and interactive elements. These tools can help capture students' attention and make the learning experience more engaging.

Teachers can also use multimedia tools like videos, podcasts, and animations to supplement their lessons. These resources can provide additional explanations, real-life examples, and different perspectives on the topic being taught. By incorporating multimedia, teachers can cater to different learning styles and make the content more accessible and relatable to students.

5.4.2 Online Collaborative Platforms

TECHNOLOGY HAS MADE it easier than ever for students to collaborate and work together, regardless of their physical location. Online collaborative platforms such as Google Docs, Microsoft Teams, and Padlet allow students to collaborate on projects, share ideas, and provide feedback in real-time. These platforms promote teamwork, communication, and critical thinking skills as students learn to work together towards a common goal.

Teachers can create collaborative activities where students work in groups to solve problems, analyze data, or create presentations. By using these online platforms, students can actively participate in the learning process, share their thoughts, and learn from their peers. This fosters a sense of community and encourages students to take ownership of their learning.

5.4.3 Gamification and Educational Apps

GAMIFICATION IS A POWERFUL tool that can be used to motivate and engage students in the learning process. By incorporating elements of games, such as points, badges, and leaderboards, teachers can create a fun and competitive learning environment. Educational apps and online platforms like Kahoot, Quizlet, and Classcraft allow teachers to gamify their lessons and assess students' understanding in an interactive and engaging way.

Teachers can create quizzes, flashcards, and interactive games that align with the curriculum and learning objectives. These activities not only make learning more enjoyable but also provide immediate feedback to students, allowing them to track their progress and identify areas for improvement. Gamification can also foster a sense of achievement and encourage students to take an active role in their learning journey.

5.4.4 Virtual Reality and Augmented Reality

VIRTUAL REALITY (VR) and augmented reality (AR) are emerging technologies that have the potential to revolutionize the way we learn. VR immerses students in a virtual environment, allowing them to explore places, historical events, or scientific concepts that would otherwise be inaccessible. AR overlays digital content onto the real world, enhancing students' understanding and interaction with their surroundings.

Teachers can use VR and AR to create virtual field trips, simulations, and interactive experiences that bring the curriculum to life. For example, students can explore ancient civilizations, dissect virtual organisms, or conduct virtual experiments. These technologies provide a unique and immersive learning experience, making complex concepts more tangible and memorable for students.

5.4.5 Online Discussion Forums and Social Media

ONLINE DISCUSSION FORUMS and social media platforms can be powerful tools for promoting collaboration, critical thinking, and communication skills. Teachers can create online discussion forums using platforms like Edmodo,

Schoology, or Google Classroom, where students can engage in meaningful discussions, ask questions, and share resources.

Social media platforms like Twitter, Instagram, and Facebook can also be used to facilitate discussions and share resources with students. Teachers can create class hashtags or groups where students can post their thoughts, ask questions, and share relevant articles or videos. These platforms provide an opportunity for students to connect with their peers, engage in discussions beyond the classroom, and develop their digital citizenship skills.

5.4.6 Personalized Learning Platforms

TECHNOLOGY CAN ALSO be used to personalize the learning experience for students. Personalized learning platforms like Khan Academy, Duolingo, and IXL provide students with individualized learning paths based on their strengths, weaknesses, and learning preferences. These platforms use algorithms to adapt the content and pace of instruction to meet each student's needs.

Teachers can incorporate personalized learning platforms into their teaching by assigning specific activities or modules to students based on their individual needs. This allows students to learn at their own pace, receive immediate feedback, and track their progress. Personalized learning platforms can help students develop self-directed learning skills and foster a sense of autonomy and ownership over their education.

Incorporating technology into the classroom can open up a world of possibilities for both teachers and students. By leveraging the power of technology, teachers can create interactive and engaging learning experiences that cater to the diverse needs and interests of their students. However, it is important to remember that technology should be used as a tool to enhance teaching and learning rather than replace the human connection and interaction that are essential for transformative teaching.

Chapter 6: The Ripple Effect

6.1 Creating a Positive Impact on Students

As a teacher, one of the most rewarding aspects of your role is the opportunity to make a positive impact on your students' lives. Each day, you have the power to inspire, motivate, and guide them towards personal and academic growth. In this section, we will explore various strategies and approaches that can help you create a lasting and positive impact on your students.

6.1.1 Building Meaningful Relationships

BUILDING MEANINGFUL relationships with your students is the foundation for creating a positive impact. When students feel valued, respected, and understood, they are more likely to engage in the learning process and take risks in their academic pursuits. Take the time to get to know your students on a personal level, showing genuine interest in their lives, hobbies, and aspirations. By establishing a connection with each student, you can tailor your teaching approach to their individual needs and interests, fostering a sense of belonging and trust within the classroom.

6.1.2 Cultivating a Growth Mindset

ENCOURAGING A GROWTH mindset in your students can have a profound impact on their learning and development. Teach them that intelligence and abilities can be developed through effort, perseverance, and a willingness to learn from mistakes. By praising their efforts and highlighting their progress, rather than solely focusing on outcomes, you can instill a sense of resilience and a belief in their own potential. This mindset will empower them to embrace challenges, overcome obstacles, and continuously strive for improvement.

6.1.3 Providing Constructive Feedback

FEEDBACK IS A POWERFUL tool for growth and improvement. When providing feedback to your students, it is essential to be specific, constructive, and supportive. Focus on highlighting their strengths and areas for improvement, offering actionable suggestions for growth. Encourage self-reflection and self-assessment, helping students develop the skills to evaluate their own work critically. By providing timely and meaningful feedback, you can guide your students towards achieving their goals and foster a culture of continuous learning.

6.1.4 Creating a Safe and Inclusive Learning Environment

A SAFE AND INCLUSIVE learning environment is crucial for students to thrive academically and emotionally. Foster a classroom culture that celebrates diversity, promotes respect, and values open dialogue. Encourage students to express their thoughts and opinions, creating a space where everyone feels heard and valued. Address any instances of bullying or discrimination promptly and firmly, ensuring that all students feel safe and supported. By creating an inclusive environment, you can empower your students to embrace their unique identities and perspectives, fostering a sense of belonging and acceptance.

6.1.5 Encouraging Student Autonomy and Ownership

EMPOWERING STUDENTS to take ownership of their learning is a powerful way to create a positive impact. Provide opportunities for student choice and autonomy, allowing them to explore their interests and passions within the curriculum. Foster a sense of responsibility by involving students in decision-making processes, such as setting classroom rules or designing projects. By giving students a voice and agency in their education, you can ignite their intrinsic motivation and cultivate a lifelong love for learning.

6.1.6 Inspiring a Love for Learning

AS A TRANSFORMATIVE teacher, your ultimate goal is to inspire a love for learning in your students. Create a classroom environment that is engaging, stimulating, and filled with curiosity. Incorporate hands-on activities, real-world connections, and interdisciplinary approaches to make learning meaningful and relevant. Foster a sense of wonder and excitement, encouraging students to ask questions, explore new ideas, and think critically. By nurturing a love for learning, you can empower your students to become lifelong learners who are curious, adaptable, and eager to make a positive impact on the world.

6.1.7 Modeling Empathy and Compassion

AS AN EDUCATOR, YOU have the opportunity to model empathy and compassion for your students. Show genuine care and concern for their well-being, both academically and emotionally. Demonstrate kindness, understanding, and patience in your interactions with students, creating a supportive and nurturing environment. Teach your students the importance of empathy and encourage them to practice acts of kindness towards one another. By modeling empathy and compassion, you can inspire your students to develop these essential qualities and create a positive ripple effect in their own lives and the lives of others.

In conclusion, creating a positive impact on students goes beyond academic achievement. It involves building meaningful relationships, cultivating a growth mindset, providing constructive feedback, creating a safe and inclusive learning environment, encouraging student autonomy, inspiring a love for learning, and modeling empathy and compassion. By implementing these strategies, you can transform your teaching practice and make a lasting difference in the lives of your students. Remember, the impact you have on your students today can shape their future and contribute to a more compassionate and inclusive society.

6.2 Fostering Empathy and Compassion

EMPATHY AND COMPASSION are essential qualities that teachers can cultivate in themselves and their students. By fostering empathy and compassion, teachers can create a classroom environment that promotes understanding, kindness, and respect. In this section, we will explore various strategies and activities that can help teachers foster empathy and compassion in their students.

6.2.1 Modeling Empathy and Compassion

ONE OF THE MOST EFFECTIVE ways to foster empathy and compassion in students is by modeling these qualities ourselves as teachers. When students see their teachers demonstrating empathy and compassion towards others, they are more likely to internalize these values and exhibit them in their own interactions.

Teachers can model empathy and compassion by actively listening to students, showing genuine interest in their thoughts and feelings, and responding with understanding and kindness. Additionally, teachers can share personal stories or examples that highlight the importance of empathy and compassion in their own lives. By doing so, teachers create a safe space for students to express their emotions and develop their own empathetic and compassionate behaviors.

6.2.2 Promoting Perspective-Taking

PERSPECTIVE-TAKING is a crucial skill that allows individuals to understand and empathize with the experiences and emotions of others. Teachers can promote perspective-taking by incorporating activities and discussions that encourage students to consider different viewpoints and understand the impact of their actions on others.

One effective strategy is to assign students to take on different roles in a scenario or debate. By stepping into someone else's shoes, students gain a deeper understanding of the emotions and perspectives of others. Teachers can also use literature, films, or real-life examples to spark discussions about empathy and compassion. These discussions can help students develop a broader perspective and cultivate empathy for people from diverse backgrounds and experiences.

6.2.3 Encouraging Acts of Kindness

ACTS OF KINDNESS HAVE a powerful impact on both the giver and the receiver. Teachers can create a culture of kindness in the classroom by encouraging students to perform acts of kindness towards their peers, teachers, and the wider community. This can be done through structured activities such as a kindness challenge or random acts of kindness.

Teachers can also incorporate service-learning projects into their curriculum, where students engage in activities that benefit others in need. These projects provide students with opportunities to develop empathy and compassion by actively participating in acts of service and understanding the impact of their actions on others.

6.2.4 Cultivating a Culture of Inclusion

CREATING A CULTURE of inclusion is essential for fostering empathy and compassion in the classroom. Teachers can promote inclusivity by celebrating diversity, respecting individual differences, and creating opportunities for students to learn about different cultures, backgrounds, and perspectives.

Inclusive classroom practices can include using diverse teaching materials, incorporating multicultural literature, and inviting guest speakers from various backgrounds to share their experiences. Teachers can also facilitate discussions and activities that promote understanding and respect for different identities and perspectives. By creating an inclusive environment, teachers empower students to develop empathy and compassion towards all individuals, regardless of their differences.

6.2.5 Practicing Mindfulness and Self-Reflection

MINDFULNESS AND SELF-reflection are powerful tools for fostering empathy and compassion. Teachers can incorporate mindfulness practices into their daily routines, such as guided breathing exercises or moments of silence. These practices help students develop self-awareness, emotional regulation, and empathy towards themselves and others.

Self-reflection activities can also be integrated into the curriculum, where students are encouraged to reflect on their thoughts, feelings, and actions. By engaging in self-reflection, students develop a deeper understanding of their own emotions and the impact of their behavior on others. This process promotes empathy and compassion by encouraging students to consider the perspectives and feelings of those around them.

6.2.6 Collaborative Learning and Cooperative Activities

COLLABORATIVE LEARNING and cooperative activities provide students with opportunities to work together, solve problems, and develop empathy and compassion towards their peers. Teachers can design group projects, discussions, and problem-solving activities that require students to listen to each other, respect different opinions, and work towards a common goal.

Through collaborative learning, students learn to appreciate the strengths and contributions of their peers, develop empathy for their struggles, and practice compassion by offering support and assistance. These experiences foster a sense of community and empathy within the classroom, creating a positive and inclusive learning environment.

6.2.7 Reflecting on Empathy and Compassion

REGULAR REFLECTION on empathy and compassion is essential for students to internalize these qualities and make them a part of their daily lives. Teachers can incorporate reflection activities into their lessons, such as journaling, group discussions, or individual reflections.

During these reflection activities, students can consider how they have demonstrated empathy and compassion, reflect on the impact of their actions on others, and identify areas for growth. By encouraging students to reflect on their experiences, teachers reinforce the importance of empathy and compassion and provide opportunities for students to develop these qualities further.

Fostering empathy and compassion in the classroom is a transformative process that benefits both students and teachers. By modeling empathy, promoting perspective-taking, encouraging acts of kindness, cultivating a culture of inclusion, practicing mindfulness and self-reflection, facilitating collaborative learning, and promoting regular reflection, teachers can create a classroom environment that nurtures empathy and compassion in all its members. Through these efforts, teachers can empower students to become compassionate and empathetic individuals who contribute positively to their communities and the world.

6.3 Inspiring Lifelong Learning

INSPIRING LIFELONG learning is a fundamental goal of transformative teaching. As educators, we have the power to ignite a passion for learning within our students that extends far beyond the walls of the classroom. By fostering a love for learning, we can empower our students to become lifelong learners who are curious, motivated, and eager to explore the world around them.

6.3.1 Cultivating Curiosity

CURIOSITY IS THE SPARK that ignites the flame of lifelong learning. It is the desire to explore, question, and seek knowledge. As transformative teachers, we can cultivate curiosity in our students by creating an environment that encourages exploration and inquiry. We can do this by:

- Encouraging questions: Welcoming and valuing students' questions, no matter how simple or complex, fosters a sense of curiosity and promotes active engagement in the learning process. By providing opportunities for students to ask questions and seek answers, we can nurture their natural curiosity.

- Providing real-world connections: Making connections between the content being taught and real-world applications helps students see the relevance and importance of what they are learning.

By showing them how the knowledge and skills they acquire in the classroom can be applied in their everyday lives, we can inspire them to continue learning beyond the classroom.

• Offering choice and autonomy: Allowing students to have a say in their learning and providing them with choices empowers them to take ownership of their education. When students have the freedom to explore topics that interest them and pursue their own lines of inquiry, they are more likely to develop a genuine love for learning.

6.3.2 Fostering a Growth Mindset

A GROWTH MINDSET IS the belief that abilities and intelligence can be developed through dedication, effort, and perseverance. By fostering a growth mindset in our students, we can instill in them the belief that they can continue to learn and grow throughout their lives. Here are some strategies for fostering a growth mindset:

• Emphasizing effort and progress: Instead of focusing solely on grades or final outcomes, we can shift the focus to the effort students put into their learning and the progress they make along the way. By celebrating their growth and highlighting the importance of perseverance and resilience, we can inspire them to continue learning and pushing themselves.

• Providing constructive feedback: Offering specific and constructive feedback that focuses on areas for improvement rather than simply pointing out mistakes helps students see feedback as an opportunity for growth. By providing guidance and support, we can help them develop the skills and strategies they need to overcome challenges and continue learning.

• Modeling a growth mindset: As teachers, we are role models for our students. By demonstrating a growth mindset in our own learning and sharing our own struggles and successes, we can inspire them to adopt a similar mindset. When students see that even their teacher is constantly learning and growing, they are more likely to believe in their own ability to do the same.

6.3.3 Promoting Self-Directed Learning

SELF-DIRECTED LEARNING is the ability to take responsibility for one's own learning and to actively seek out knowledge and skills independently. By promoting self-directed learning, we can empower our students to become independent learners who are motivated and capable of pursuing their own interests and passions. Here are some strategies for promoting self-directed learning:

• Encouraging goal-setting: Helping students set goals for their learning and providing them with the tools and resources they need to achieve those goals can foster a sense of autonomy and self-direction. By guiding them in setting realistic and achievable goals, we can support their journey towards becoming self-directed learners.

• Teaching metacognitive skills: Metacognition refers to the ability to think about one's own thinking and learning processes. By teaching students metacognitive skills such as self-reflection, self-assessment, and self-regulation, we can help them become more aware of their own learning needs and strategies. This awareness empowers them to take control of their learning and make informed decisions about how to best approach their studies.

• Providing opportunities for independent exploration: Creating opportunities for students to pursue their own interests and passions through independent projects, research, or creative endeavors allows them to take ownership of their learning. By providing guidance and support, we can help them develop the skills and confidence they need to explore new topics and ideas on their own.

6.3.4 Nurturing a Love for Reading

READING IS A GATEWAY to lifelong learning. By nurturing a love for reading in our students, we can open up a world of knowledge and imagination for them to explore. Here are some strategies for nurturing a love for reading:

- Creating a reading-friendly environment: Designing a classroom environment that is inviting and conducive to reading can help foster a love for books. Providing comfortable reading spaces, a variety of reading materials, and opportunities for independent reading can encourage students to develop a reading habit.

- Sharing a variety of genres and authors: Exposing students to a wide range of genres, authors, and styles of writing can help them discover their own reading preferences and interests. By introducing them to diverse voices and perspectives, we can broaden their horizons and inspire them to explore different genres and authors.

- Engaging in book discussions: Encouraging students to share their thoughts, ideas, and reactions to the books they read can deepen their engagement with the text and foster a sense of community around reading. By facilitating book discussions and providing opportunities for students to recommend books to their peers, we can create a culture of reading in the classroom.

Inspiring lifelong learning is a journey that requires dedication, passion, and a commitment to continuous growth. As transformative teachers, we have the power to shape the future by instilling in our students a love for learning that will stay with them throughout their lives. By cultivating curiosity, fostering a growth mindset, promoting self-directed learning, and nurturing a love for reading, we can inspire our students to become lifelong learners who are eager to explore, discover, and make a positive impact on the world.

6.4 Promoting Social Change and Advocacy

AS EDUCATORS, WE HAVE the power to not only shape the minds of our students but also to inspire them to become agents of social change and advocates for a better world. In this section, we will explore how teachers can promote social change and advocacy within the classroom and beyond.

6.4.1 Fostering Social Awareness

ONE OF THE FIRST STEPS in promoting social change and advocacy is fostering social awareness among our students. By helping them understand and empathize with the experiences of others, we can ignite a sense of compassion and a desire to make a difference. Here are some strategies to foster social awareness:

1. **Cultivate a diverse and inclusive classroom**: Create a classroom environment that celebrates diversity and encourages students to appreciate and respect different cultures, backgrounds, and perspectives. Incorporate diverse literature, guest speakers, and discussions that explore social issues.

2. **Engage in community service**: Encourage students to actively participate in community service projects that address local social issues. This hands-on experience allows them to see the impact they can make and develop a sense of responsibility towards their community.

3. **Explore current events**: Discuss current events and social issues with your students, encouraging them to critically analyze and

reflect on the world around them. Help them understand the root causes of these issues and brainstorm possible solutions.

6.4.2 Empowering Student Voice

EMPOWERING STUDENTS to use their voice is essential to promoting social change and advocacy. By providing them with opportunities to express their opinions and take action, we can instill a sense of agency and empower them to make a difference. Here are some ways to empower student voices:

1. **Classroom discussions and debates**: Create a safe space for students to express their opinions and engage in respectful debates. Encourage them to research and present their arguments on various social issues, allowing them to develop critical thinking and communication skills.

2. **Student-led initiatives**: Support and guide students in initiating their own projects or campaigns that address social issues they are passionate about. This could include organizing fundraisers, awareness campaigns, or community events.

3. **Digital platforms**: Utilize technology to amplify student voices. Encourage them to create blogs, podcasts, or social media campaigns to raise awareness about social issues and advocate for change.

6.4.3 Collaborating with the Community

COLLABORATING WITH the community is crucial to promoting social change and advocacy. By connecting students with local organizations and individuals working towards social justice, we can provide them with real-world experiences and opportunities to make a meaningful impact. Here are some ways to collaborate with the community:

1. **Guest speakers and field trips**: Invite guest speakers from local organizations or activists to share their experiences and insights with your students. Organize field trips to community centers, non-profit organizations, or local events that focus on social issues.

2. **Partnerships with local organizations**: Establish partnerships with local organizations that align with your classroom goals and values. This could involve volunteering together, participating in community events, or collaborating on projects that address social issues.

3. **Service-learning projects**: Engage students in service-learning projects that involve collaborating with community members to address social issues. This hands-on approach allows students to apply their knowledge and skills while making a positive impact in the community.

6.4.4 Integrating Social Change into the Curriculum

INTEGRATING SOCIAL change and advocacy into the curriculum ensures that these important topics are not treated as separate from academic learning but rather as integral components of education. Here are some ways to integrate social change into the curriculum:

1. **Project-based learning**: Design projects that require students to research, analyze, and propose solutions to real-world social issues. This interdisciplinary approach allows students to apply

their knowledge and skills to make a tangible impact.

2. **Literature and media**: Incorporate literature, films, and other media that explore social issues and promote empathy and understanding. Use these resources as a springboard for discussion and critical analysis.

3. **Cross-curricular connections**: Collaborate with colleagues from different subject areas to create interdisciplinary units that address social issues. This allows students to see the interconnectedness of various subjects and encourages them to think critically and creatively.

By promoting social change and advocacy within the classroom, we can empower our students to become active participants in shaping a more just and equitable society. Through fostering social awareness, empowering student voices, collaborating with the community, and integrating social change into the curriculum, we can inspire the next generation of changemakers. Let us continue to use our ink and hearts to create a ripple effect that transforms not only our classrooms but also the world around us.

Chapter7: Closing the Book, Opening Hearts

7.1 Reflecting on Teaching Practices

REFLECTING ON OUR TEACHING practices is an essential part of professional growth and development. It allows us to assess our strengths and areas for improvement, make adjustments to our teaching strategies, and ultimately enhance the learning experience for our students. In this section, we will explore the importance of reflection, different methods of reflection, and how to effectively implement reflection into our teaching practices.

7.1.1 The Power of Reflection

REFLECTION IS A POWERFUL tool that enables us to gain insights into our teaching practices and their impact on students. It allows us to step back and critically analyze our instructional methods, classroom management techniques, and overall approach to teaching. By reflecting on our experiences, we can identify what worked well and what could be improved, leading to more effective teaching strategies.

When we engage in reflective practices, we become more aware of our teaching style, strengths, and areas for growth. This self-awareness is crucial for professional development, as it helps us identify areas where we can enhance our skills and knowledge. Additionally, reflection allows us to connect theory with practice, bridging the gap between educational research and our classroom realities.

7.1.2 Methods of Reflection

THERE ARE VARIOUS METHODS of reflection that teachers can employ to gain valuable insights into their teaching practices. Here are a few commonly used methods:

Journaling

KEEPING A REFLECTIVE journal is a popular method for teachers to document their thoughts, experiences, and observations. By regularly writing in a journal, teachers can reflect on their daily interactions with students, instructional strategies, and classroom dynamics. This process allows for deeper self-reflection and provides a written record of growth over time.

Peer observation and feedback

ENGAGING IN PEER OBSERVATION and feedback is another effective method of reflection. By observing our colleagues' teaching practices and receiving constructive feedback, we can gain new perspectives and ideas for improvement. Collaborating with fellow teachers fosters a supportive environment for professional growth and encourages the sharing of best practices.

Video Recording

RECORDING OUR TEACHING sessions and reviewing the footage can be an eye-opening experience. It allows us to observe our interactions with students, body language, and instructional techniques from an objective standpoint. By watching ourselves teach, we can identify areas where we excel and areas that need refinement.

Student Feedback

SEEKING FEEDBACK DIRECTLY from our students is a valuable method of reflection. By asking students for their input on our teaching methods, classroom environment, and learning experiences, we gain valuable insights into their perspectives. This feedback can help us make adjustments to our teaching practices to better meet the needs of our students.

7.1.3 Implementing Reflection into Teaching Practices

TO EFFECTIVELY IMPLEMENT reflection into our teaching practices, it is important to establish a routine and create a supportive environment for reflection. Here are some strategies to consider:

Schedule regular reflection time.

SET ASIDE DEDICATED time each week or month for reflection. This could be during planning periods, after school, or on weekends. By making reflection a regular part of our routine, we ensure that it becomes a consistent practice.

Create a reflection space.

DESIGNATE A SPECIFIC area in your classroom or at home as a reflection space. This could be a comfortable chair, a quiet corner, or a cozy nook. Having a designated space for reflection helps create a focused and peaceful environment for introspection.

Use prompts and guiding questions.

TO GUIDE YOUR REFLECTION process, consider using prompts or guiding questions. These can help direct your thoughts and prompt deeper reflection. For example, you could ask yourself, "What instructional strategies were most effective in engaging my students this week?" or "How did I create a positive classroom culture today?"

Engage in collaborative reflection.

COLLABORATE WITH COLLEAGUES or join a professional learning community to engage in reflective discussions. Sharing experiences, challenges, and successes with others can provide valuable insights and support. Collaborative reflection also fosters a sense of camaraderie and encourages continuous growth.

Set goals for improvement.

BASED ON YOUR REFLECTIONS, set specific goals for improvement. These goals can be focused on enhancing specific teaching strategies, classroom management techniques, or student engagement. By setting goals, you provide yourself with a clear direction for growth and development.

7.1.4 The Transformative Power of Reflection

REFLECTION HAS THE power to transform our teaching practices and create a positive impact on our students. By regularly reflecting on our teaching methods, we become more attuned to the needs of our students, develop a deeper understanding of their strengths and challenges, and refine our instructional strategies accordingly.

Through reflection, we can cultivate a more empathetic and compassionate approach to teaching, creating a safe and supportive learning environment for our students. It allows us to continuously grow as educators, adapt to the ever-changing needs of our students, and inspire a love for learning that extends beyond the classroom.

As we close this chapter on reflecting on teaching practices, let us remember that the journey of transformative teaching is an ongoing one. By embracing reflection as a vital part of our professional growth, we can continue to evolve as educators and make a lasting impact on the hearts and minds of our students.

7.2 Celebrating Growth and Achievements

AS A TEACHER, ONE OF the most rewarding aspects of your job is witnessing the growth and achievements of your students. Throughout the school year, you have worked diligently to create a nurturing and supportive environment where your students can thrive. Now, it is time to celebrate their progress and accomplishments. In this section, we will explore various ways to celebrate growth and achievements in your classroom.

7.2.1 Recognizing Individual Achievements

EVERY STUDENT IS UNIQUE, and each one has their own set of strengths and talents. It is important to recognize and celebrate the individual achievements of your students. This can be done through verbal praise, written notes, or certificates of achievement. Take the time to acknowledge their hard work and effort, and let them know that their accomplishments are valued.

7.2.2 Showcasing Student Work

DISPLAYING STUDENT work is a powerful way to celebrate their growth and achievements. Create a designated space in your classroom where students can proudly showcase their projects, artwork, or written assignments. This not only boosts their confidence but also allows their peers to appreciate and learn from their work. Consider organizing a class exhibition or inviting parents to a showcase event to further highlight their accomplishments.

7.2.3 Personal Reflections

ENCOURAGE YOUR STUDENTS to reflect on their own growth and achievements throughout the year. Provide them with opportunities to write personal reflections or create visual representations of their progress. This can be done through journaling, creating scrapbooks, or even making short videos. By reflecting on their journey, students gain a deeper understanding of their own growth and can take pride in their accomplishments.

7.2.4 Group Celebrations

IN ADDITION TO RECOGNIZING individual achievements, it is important to celebrate the collective growth of your class as a whole. Plan group celebrations to acknowledge milestones and accomplishments reached by the entire class. This can be as simple as a class party or a special activity that the students have been looking forward to. By celebrating together, students develop a sense of camaraderie and learn the value of teamwork and collaboration.

7.2.5 Inviting Guest Speakers

BRINGING IN GUEST SPEAKERS who have achieved success in various fields can be a great way to inspire and motivate your students. These individuals can share their own stories of growth and achievement, providing valuable insights and advice. Whether it is a successful entrepreneur, an accomplished artist, or a community leader, guest speakers can offer a fresh perspective and serve as role models for your students.

7.2.6 Awards and Recognition

CONSIDER IMPLEMENTING an awards system to recognize outstanding achievements in your classroom. This can be done on a monthly or quarterly basis, where students are nominated for various categories such as academic excellence, leadership, creativity, or perseverance. Awards can be presented during a special ceremony or assembly, creating a sense of excitement and pride among the students.

7.2.7 Parent Involvement

INVOLVING PARENTS IN celebrating their child's growth and achievements is essential. Keep parents informed about their child's progress throughout the year through regular communication channels such as newsletters, emails, or parent-teacher conferences. Additionally, consider organizing parent appreciation events where students can showcase their work and parents can actively participate in celebrating their child's accomplishments.

7.2.8 Community Engagement

EXTEND THE CELEBRATION of growth and achievements beyond the classroom by involving the wider community. Collaborate with local businesses, organizations, or community leaders to create opportunities for students to showcase their work or talents. This can include art exhibitions, performances, or community service projects. By engaging with the community, students gain a sense of pride in their accomplishments and understand the impact they can have on the world around them.

7.2.9 Reflection and Gratitude

AS THE SCHOOL YEAR comes to a close, take the time to reflect on the growth and achievements of both yourself and your students. Consider writing personal notes of gratitude to each student, highlighting their individual progress, and expressing your appreciation for their efforts. Encourage your students to reflect on their own growth and express gratitude for the support they have received throughout the year. This practice of reflection and gratitude fosters a positive and appreciative mindset, setting the stage for continued growth and success in the future.

Celebrating the growth and achievements of your students is a powerful way to reinforce their self-confidence, motivation, and love for learning. By creating a culture of celebration in your classroom, you not only acknowledge their accomplishments but also inspire them to reach even greater heights. So, let the confetti fly, the balloons soar, and the applause resound as you celebrate the remarkable journey of growth and achievement that you and your students have embarked upon together.

7.3 Saying Goodbye to Students

AS A TEACHER, SAYING goodbye to your students at the end of the school year can be bittersweet. You have spent months building relationships, fostering growth, and creating a safe and nurturing environment for learning. Now, it is time to bid farewell to the students who have become a part of your daily life. Saying goodbye is not just a formality; it is an opportunity to leave a lasting impression and ensure that your students feel valued and appreciated. In this section, we will explore some meaningful ways to say goodbye to your students and leave them with a sense of gratitude and inspiration.

7.3.1 Reflecting on the Journey

BEFORE SAYING GOODBYE, take some time to reflect on the journey you and your students have embarked on together. Think about the progress they have made, the challenges they have overcome, and the moments of joy and growth you have shared. Reflecting on these experiences will help you appreciate the impact you have had on your students' lives and remind you of the meaningful connections you have made.

7.3.2 Expressing Gratitude

EXPRESSING GRATITUDE is a powerful way to say goodbye to your students. Take the time to write personalized thank-you notes to each student, highlighting their unique strengths and contributions to the classroom community. Let them know how much you appreciate their hard work, dedication, and growth throughout the year. By acknowledging their efforts, you are not only showing gratitude but also boosting their self-esteem and confidence.

7.3.3 Sharing Memories

CREATE A SPACE WHERE students can share their favorite memories from the school year. Set up a memory board or a digital platform where students can write or record their most cherished moments. Encourage them to reflect on their personal growth, friendships formed, and the lessons they have learned. This activity allows students to celebrate their achievements and provides a sense of closure as they prepare to move on to the next grade.

7.3.4 Farewell Ceremony

ORGANIZE A FAREWELL ceremony to honor your students' accomplishments and bid them a proper goodbye. This can be a formal event or a more casual gathering, depending on your students' age and preferences. During the ceremony, take the time to recognize each student individually, highlighting their strengths and growth throughout the year. You can also invite parents and other teachers to share their thoughts and memories of the students. This ceremony not only celebrates the students' achievements but also creates a sense of closure and unity within the classroom community.

7.3.5 Time Capsule

CREATE A TIME CAPSULE with your students to capture their memories and aspirations. Have each student write a letter to their future selves, reflecting on their experiences, goals, and dreams. Encourage them to include mementos or photographs that hold special meaning to them. Seal the time capsule and set a date in the future when it will be opened. This activity allows students to reflect on their growth and provides them with a tangible reminder of their time in your classroom.

7.3.6 Inspiring Words

BEFORE SAYING GOODBYE, share some inspiring words with your students. Reflect on the lessons they have learned, the challenges they have overcome, and the potential you see in each of them. Encourage them to continue pursuing their dreams, embracing new opportunities, and making a positive impact on the world. Your words of encouragement and inspiration will stay with them long after they leave your classroom.

7.3.7 Staying connected

SAYING GOODBYE DOES not mean severing all ties with your students. Encourage them to stay connected with you and their classmates through social media, email, or a class newsletter. Let them know that you are always there to support and guide them, even after they have moved on to the next grade. By maintaining a connection, you can continue to be a source of inspiration and mentorship for your students.

7.3.8 Leaving a Lasting Legacy

AS YOU SAY GOODBYE to your students, consider leaving a lasting legacy behind. This could be a project, a tradition, or a set of values that will continue to shape the classroom community even after you are gone. By leaving a legacy, you ensure that your impact as a teacher extends beyond the time you spend with your students. It is a way to inspire future generations and create a sense of continuity in the classroom.

Saying goodbye to your students is an emotional and significant moment in a teacher's journey. By reflecting on the journey, expressing gratitude, sharing memories, and leaving a lasting legacy, you can ensure that your students feel valued, appreciated, and inspired as they move on to new adventures. Remember, the impact you have had on their lives will continue to shape their future long after they have left your classroom.

7.4: Leaving a Lasting Legacy

AS A TEACHER, YOUR impact goes far beyond the classroom walls. The time you spend with your students leaves a lasting impression on their lives, shaping their future and influencing the world they will create. Leaving a lasting legacy is about making a difference that extends beyond the academic knowledge you impart. It is about instilling values, inspiring change, and empowering your students to become compassionate, responsible, and engaged members of society.

7.4.1 Instilling Values

ONE OF THE MOST IMPORTANT ways to leave a lasting legacy is by instilling values in your students. Education is not just about acquiring knowledge; it is also about developing character and integrity. Take the time to explicitly teach and model values such as empathy, respect, kindness, and perseverance. Create opportunities for your students to practice these values in real-life situations, both inside and outside the classroom. By consistently reinforcing these values, you are helping to shape the moral compass of your students and preparing them to make ethical decisions in the future.

7.4.2 Inspiring Change

AS A TRANSFORMATIVE teacher, you have the power to inspire change in your students. Encourage them to think critically, question the status quo, and challenge societal norms. Help them develop a sense of agency and empower them to take action on issues that matter to them. Provide opportunities for them to engage in service-learning projects, community initiatives, and advocacy work. By nurturing their sense of social responsibility, you are equipping them with the tools to make a positive impact on the world around them.

7.4.3 Fostering Lifelong Learning

LEAVING A LASTING LEGACY also means fostering a love for learning that extends beyond the classroom. Help your students develop a growth mindset by encouraging them to embrace challenges, persevere through setbacks, and view mistakes as opportunities for growth. Teach them how to set goals, develop effective study habits, and seek out resources independently. By instilling a passion for learning, you are empowering your students to become lifelong learners who will continue to grow and thrive long after they leave your classroom.

7.4.4 Promoting Social Change and Advocacy

ONE OF THE MOST POWERFUL ways to leave a lasting legacy is by promoting social change and advocacy. Teach your students about social justice issues, inequality, and the importance of standing up for what is right. Encourage them to use their voices to advocate for those who are marginalized or oppressed. Provide them with opportunities to engage in meaningful discussions, debates, and projects that address real-world problems. By empowering your students to become agents of change, you are helping to create a more just and equitable society.

7.4.5 Building Connections and Networks

LEAVING A LASTING LEGACY also involves building connections and networks that will support your students beyond the classroom. Encourage your students to build relationships with their peers, mentors, and professionals in their fields of interest. Help them develop networking skills, such as effective communication, active listening, and professional etiquette. Provide opportunities for them to connect with alumni, industry experts, and community leaders. By helping your students build strong networks, you are opening doors for their future success and creating a support system that will guide them throughout their lives.

7.4.6 Documenting and Sharing Success Stories

TO LEAVE A LASTING legacy, it is important to document and share the success stories of your students. Keep a record of their achievements, both academic and personal. Showcase their growth, progress, and accomplishments through portfolios, exhibitions, or digital platforms. Share these stories with your current and future students, as well as with parents, colleagues, and the wider community. By celebrating the successes of your students, you are not only validating their hard work but also inspiring others to strive for excellence.

7.4.7 Continuing Professional Development

LEAVING A LASTING LEGACY also involves your own professional growth and development. Stay updated with the latest research, teaching strategies, and educational trends. Attend conferences, workshops, and seminars to expand your knowledge and skills. Share your expertise with colleagues through professional learning communities, mentoring programs, or by presenting at conferences. By continuously improving yourself as an educator, you are setting an example for your students and contributing to the advancement of the teaching profession as a whole.

7.4.8 Staying Connected with Former Students

EVEN AFTER YOUR STUDENTS leave your classroom, it is important to stay connected with them. Maintain open lines of communication through social media, email, or alumni networks. Celebrate their milestones, offer guidance and support when needed, and continue to be a source of inspiration and encouragement. By staying connected with your former students, you are not only nurturing lifelong relationships but also creating a network of individuals who can support and uplift each other throughout their lives.

Leaving a lasting legacy as a teacher is about more than just the knowledge you impart. It is about instilling values, inspiring change, fostering lifelong learning, promoting social change, building connections, documenting success stories, continuing professional development, and staying connected with former students. By embracing these principles, you can make a profound and lasting impact on the lives of your students, shaping them into compassionate, responsible, and engaged individuals who will go on to create a better world.

Conclution:

Embracing the Transformative Power of Emotions in Education

"Ink and Heart: A Guide to Transformative Teaching—Where Emotions Meet Chalk Dust" has taken us on a profound exploration of the transformative power of emotions in the realm of education. We have delved into the heart of teaching, recognizing the crucial role that emotions play in creating meaningful learning experiences. Throughout this journey, we have discovered the immense potential for growth, connection, and personal transformation that arises when we embrace the intersection of emotions and knowledge.

In this concluding chapter, we reflect on the transformative journey we have embarked upon and the key insights we have gained along the way. We are reminded that teaching is not simply a transactional exchange of information but a deeply human endeavor that requires us to engage with our students on an emotional level. The art of transformative teaching lies in recognizing and harnessing the power of emotions to create an environment where students feel seen, heard, and valued.

We have explored the importance of cultivating emotional intelligence within ourselves as educators, recognizing that our own emotional well-being and self-awareness directly impact our ability to connect with and support our students. By developing empathy, practicing active listening, and embracing vulnerability, we create a safe haven where students can explore, question, and grow.

Crucial to transformative teaching is the creation of a safe and nurturing classroom environment. We have delved into strategies for establishing trust, fostering inclusivity, and promoting a sense of belonging among students. When students feel safe expressing themselves authentically, they are more likely to engage deeply in the learning process, take risks, and develop a growth mindset.

We have also explored the transformative power of emotions in the learning experience itself. Emotions are not distractions to be suppressed but valuable guides that can enhance learning and retention. By incorporating meaningful and relevant experiences, embracing storytelling, and infusing creativity into our lessons, we tap into the emotional core of our students, igniting their curiosity, passion, and intrinsic motivation.

Throughout this book, we have acknowledged the challenges and complexities that arise when emotions are brought into the educational space. We have explored strategies for managing and regulating emotions, addressing conflicts, and creating a supportive community of learners. By fostering open communication, empathy, and a culture of respect, we can navigate challenges and transform them into opportunities for growth and understanding.

"Ink and Heart: A Guide to Transformative Teaching—Where Emotions Meet Chalk Dust" serves as a reminder that transformative teaching is not a destination but a continuous journey. It calls upon us as educators to be lifelong learners, constantly reflecting on our practices, seeking new insights, and adapting to the evolving needs of our students. It reminds us that the transformative power of emotions extends beyond the classroom walls, shaping not only our students' educational experiences but also their lives as a whole.

As we conclude this transformative journey, let us carry forward the understanding that emotions are not separate from the learning process but an integral part of it. Let us embrace the complexity, messiness, and beauty of the human experience, recognizing that it is within this rich tapestry of emotions that true transformation occurs.

May "Ink and Heart: A Guide to Transformative Teaching—Where Emotions Meet Chalk Dust" serve as a guiding light, inspiring educators to embrace the power of emotions in their practice. May it fuel a passion for transformative teaching, where hearts and minds converge and students are empowered to reach their full potential.

Let us continue on this journey of transformative teaching, where emotions and knowledge intertwine and classrooms become vibrant spaces of growth, connection, and profound personal transformation. Embrace the transformative power of emotions, and may your teaching be a testament to the incredible impact we can make when we nurture the hearts and minds of our students.

Also by imed el arbi

Metamorphosis Mindset: Transforming Your Life, One Thought at a Time
Life Mastery: a Toolkit for Success
Your Hidden Power of Mind: Unleashing Your Full Potential
Rise to Radiance
Realize Your Ultimate Potential
Revitalize Your Reality: The Art of Life Transformation
Transforming Within: A Path to Personal Evolution

YouTube Secrets
YouTube Secrets: Build a Successful Channel in 5 Days
YouTube Secrets: Build a Successful Channel with Artificial Intelligence
YouTube Secrets: the Ultimate Guide to Creating Popular and Successful Content

Standalone
The Magical Woodland Adventure

The Secret Garden of Whispers
Timmy's Savanna Adventure
The Fisherman's Destiny
The Gathering in the Forest
The Great Adventure of a Lost Teddy
The Dinosaur Who Travels Through Time
The most beautiful stories for children
Felix's Lesson: The Love We Share
Luna the Moonchild's Dreamland Adventure
Sophie's Wish on the Wishing Star
The Adventure in the Enchanted Forest
Discover the Better Self Secret
Discover the Better Self Secret
ThePrincess and the Dragon's Surprising Bond
Blogging Manual for Beginner's
Lily and the Pixie: A Story of Kindness and Compassion
The Magic Portal
Whisker's Great Journey
Becoming Creative: The Path to Expressive Living
Elinor's Radiant Victory
Financial Amplification:How to Make More Money
Unique Discoveries in Tunisia
Mastering Your Mental Health
Chasing Dreams and Finding Magic
Habit Revolution: Mastering the Art of Building Good
Habits and Breaking Bad Ones
WordPress Mastery: Your Ultimate Website Guide
Money Mindset: How to Reprogram Your Brain for Financial
Success
Breaking Free: Uncovering Your Money Mindset

The Money Mindset Makeover: Unleashing True Financial Potential
Digital Deception: A Detective Jane Miller Mystery
The Enigma of Slytherin's Legacy
Bound by Love and Betrayal: an Immigrant's Journey
Tesla's 369 Revelation: A Journey to Spiritual Power
Silencing the Inner Critic: Unleashing Your True Potential
Smoke-Free Success: a Path to Health and Wealth
Navigating Success: 7 Principles of High Achievers
Charm 101: the Art of Wooing Women
Motivate Your Mind:Mastering Motivation for Success
Enchanting Cities: Exploring the World's Urban Treasures
How to Build a Successful Career in the Gig Economy
Mindful Living in the Digital Era
Raising Resilient Kids: a Mindful Guide to Parenting
The Compassionate Self: Cultivating Kindness Within
The Science of Happiness: The Pursuit of Joy
Freelance Writing Success: Launch, Grow, and Scale Your Career
Emotional Well-being: A Guide to Mental Health
HABITS RICH PEOPLE WON'T TELL YOU
Rich Habits, Rich Life: Mastering the Art of Wealth Building
Rising Horizons: Accelerating Business Development
The Lost City of Mythica: Uncovering Mythica's Secret
Generational Harmony: Winning Through Diversity
Alchemy of the Soul: A Roadmap to Life Transformation
Rise Strong: Embracing Resilience and Renewal
AI Riches: Unleashing the Profit Potential of Artificial Intelligence
Building Your Online Store with WooCommerce
Online Entrepreneurship: Success Roadmap

Shopify Mastery: The Ultimate Guide to E-commerce Success

Thriving Freelance: A Guide to Writing on Your Own Terms

Habit Mastery: A Simple Guide to Building Good Habits and Stopping Negative Ones

Reading Between the Gestures: A Brief Manual on Body Language

Bridges Across Cultures: Short story collection

Harmony in the Digital Jungle: Unveiling the Secrets of Home-Based Success

Cultivating Creativity: Fostering Innovation in Educational Settings

Gamification in Education: Leveling Up Learning Experiences

Mathematical Mastery: Unleashing the Power of Teaching

Smart Classrooms, Smarter Students: Navigating the AI Revolution in Education

Adapting Thinking Classrooms: Guide for Inclusive Education.

Flexible Thinking Classrooms: Enhancing Learning in Various Environments

Navigating the Pedagogical Landscape: Strategies for 21st-Century Educators

Revolutionary Teaching: Unleashing the Power of Pedagogy

Teaching for Tomorrow: Bridging Theory and Practice

Student-Centered Pedagogy for Lifelong Success

Differential pedagogy : How to distinguish individual differences between learners ?

Eternal Vitality: Mastering the Art of Longevity

Ink and Heart: A Guide to Transformative Teaching

Milton Keynes UK
Ingram Content Group UK Ltd.
UKHW011818011223
433620UK00001B/34